Customer

Relationship

Management

Systems

ROI and Results Measurement

Glen S. Petersen

Published by Strategic Sales Performance, Inc.
1061 W. 39th Street, Downers Grove, IL 60515

ISBN: 0-9669351-0-1

Printed in the United States of America

To Melinda, for thirty years of being a friend and a helpmate......

Table of Contents

Preface

One of the more controversial aspects of sales force automation has been the issue of justification. Some advocates have taken the position that sales force automation is a strategic initiative that does not require return on investment consideration while others have advocated the need for directly demonstrable results, for example, reduced head count.

Both extremes are detrimental to true success. A strictly strategic rationale typically results in a lack of discipline in linking investment to benefits. Ultimately, when senior management challenges the expenditure of funds to support the system, the sales organization will have little more than anecdotal evidence to support the benefits of the system. At that point, funding may be reduced and the system will deteriorate due to inadequate maintenance. When justification and implementation is based on strictly "hard" dollar savings, the organization essentially is trading one type of risk for another. By prioritizing and perhaps limiting applications to hard justification numbers, the organization may deploy applications that the field sales people consider being Big Brother in nature, or for someone else's benefit. The result can be a lack of buy-in and lack of use by the end user community. When this happens, it is very difficult to get the project back on track and secure the desirable return.

In general, justification and prioritization must represent a balance. Since the proper use of the system by the end user community will ultimately determine the return on investment, it is reasonable to deploy applications on the basis of sales rep perspective of desirability. This approach may defer higher return applications but it secures a foundation of usage, which is far more important.

Justification needs to be a blend of hard dollars and linkage to strategic and operational goals and objectives. The requirement of linkage creates discipline in terms of defining reasonable cause and effect relationships. Without this linkage, one is essentially hoping the system will improve performance. This linkage needs to be driven one step further in terms of establishing metrics that verify that change has occurred and is driving (contributing to) operational results. This book provides the necessary background and tools to develop such a justification. It is built on many years of practical experience in helping Fortune 1000 companies justify their systems.

These issues are not unique to sales and marketing systems; in a survey conducted by IBM of CEO's and CIO's in Fortune 1000 companies, executives were asked to list in priority order, the five things they cared about when buying software technology. The answers were as follows:
1. The software must solve strategic, "mission critical" issues.
2. The system must match the company's goals and fit the business's future direction.
3. The system must match the company's computing environment.
4. The system must be introduced seamlessly into the organization. It must be easy to buy, easy to build, and work easily with other systems.
5. The cost of system maintenance must be kept low.

These factors remain key factors to success; however, there are typically trade-offs. The justification format for a system provides a logical framework for evaluating the impact of these trade-offs.

For many companies, justification of the system tends to be one of the last things considered. It is the thrust of this book that justification should be considered immediately, particularly as it applies to representation in key planning processes. Further, the review of processes and capabilities should all be evaluated within the context of justification because this perspective will drive solutions that move the organization forward as opposed to simply automating existing processes.

My thanks go to Mr. Mike Webb of IMPAX Inc. for his review of the early draft of this book and his helpful suggestions and insight.

1

A Matchless Potential

In 1989, Moriarty and Swartz published a watershed article in the Harvard Business Review entitled *Automation to Boost Sales and Marketing*.[1] The article was significant for several reasons:

■ It brought legitimacy to the fledgling sales automation industry.

■ The article pegged sales and marketing costs at 15-35 percent of total corporate costs. A sobering number particularly when compared to direct labor costs.

■ Improvement in revenue growth from the application of marketing and sales automation was pegged at 10-30 percent.

The article placed in front of corporate America, the opportunity and challenge to increase sales while reducing costs. Since then, the industry has grown rapidly, but success has not been automatic.

It is easy to demonstrate the impact of these improvements. Consider a $200 million dollar company that has a gross margin of 50 percent and a profit contribution of 25 percent. Suppose this organization was able to raise sales and marketing productivity by 5 percent, this would increase revenue by $10 million. This increase is great, but consider the impact on profits:

$200M	$210M	Revenue
$100M	$105M	Gross Margin (50%)
$50M	$50M	Expense
$50M	$55M	Profit

---

[1] Moriarty, Rowland T. and Swartz, Gordon S., "Automation to Boost Sales and Marketing," Harvard Business Review, January-February 1989.

Thus, a five percent gain in productivity yields a 10 percent gain in profitability. There are no other areas within the organization that can drive this level of financial leverage. These results are not merely hypothetical, consider the following references:

■ Nalco Chemical experienced a $14 million increase in sales, which the company attributes to customer response to sales force automation applications.

■ Ascom Timeplex experienced a 33 percent increase in selling time and a radical reduction in proposal generation cycle time.

■ Oracle Corporation has dramatically improved organizational productivity by segmenting the selling duties between multiple functional areas. The enabling factor is their sales and marketing system.

Despite this impressive potential, many companies struggle with justification. What is the problem? A simple answer to this question is that too often, companies focus on the technology as though the technology is going to drive the results. This is analogous to senior management saying, "make it so", it does not work.

Sales is a process and improvements are derived from improving that process. Technology can be used to leverage and enhance that process and certainly technology can be leveraged to better measure the performance of that process but it contributes very little if it is not directed toward these purposes.

The frustration for many organizations is that the implementation of sales force automation requires significant resources and time. There is no doubt that the potential is there, but to effectively tap into it requires an understanding of how to leverage the technology and implement it correctly. An integral part of this task is to establish an effective basis for justification because it is a means for gaining senior management buy-in. In reality, it is very difficult to separate the topic of justification from the tools or analysis used to generate this insight; therefore, this book will address analytical techniques as well as a framework for justification.

System Boundaries

Pressures in the marketplace such as global competition, consumer resistance to price increases, mass customization, low growth markets, etc., have spawned new management strategies such as:

- Time based competition
- Customer retention
- Employee retention
- Activity based management
- Knowledge management
- Decentralization

These same pressures have blurred the traditional roles of marketing, sales, and customer service. The need to decrease cycle time, reduce cost, and respond to the market are placing increased emphasis on local decision making but at the same time requiring a capability for overall coordination.

From a technology standpoint, software solutions providers have developed products that follow the normal functional lines of authority. Therefore, sales force automation has addressed the historical role of the sales organization and the same has been true for marketing and customer service systems. However, the pressures in the market and the management strategies associated with them are all **customer centric** in nature. Thus, increasingly, companies are seeking a 360° view of their customer and increasing their ability to coordinate delivery of value to the customer. This is reflected in software providers offering integrated systems for managing marketing, sales, and customer service. The boundaries for system development therefore need to embrace these three areas and their linkage to the delivery side of the organization (manufacturing and logistics).

Having said this however, does not imply a bias toward one supplier system solutions versus "best of breed" solutions. Each situation should dictate the fit of functionality, cost, and lead-time requirements. However, the perspective of analysis and justification of systems must accept this view of the organization to effectively tap into results that provide true competitive advantage.

Customer Centric Model

If the organization is going to embrace a customer centric strategy, then it is logical that analysis starts with the customer needs and uses them to drive organizational response. In his book High Impact Sales Force Automation, Glen Petersen develops this concept and argues that the logical path for improving customer value is through the processes that directly impact the customer.[2] Central to this interface is the sales process. This concept is developed further in Chapter 9, but the following comments will help to develop the concept.

Although the interaction between a supplier and a customer often resembles the diagram in figure 1.1.

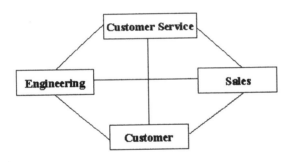

Figure 1.1 Complex interface between a supplier and a customer

It is possible to visualize these interactions taking place in the context of the sales process as indicated in figure 1.2.

Figure 1.2 is not meant to imply that every interaction passes through the sales process, it does however imply that all interactions can be viewed as **supporting** the sales process. The model used for system justification will use this concept as its foundation.

---

[2] Petersen, Glen S. *High Impact Sales Force Automation*, Boca Raton: St. Lucie Press, 1997.

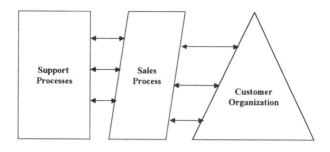

Figure 1.2 Support processes as an extension of the sales process

A Model For Justification

The model used for justification within this book will address the hierarchy of goals within the organization. This hierarchy is reflected in figure 1.3.

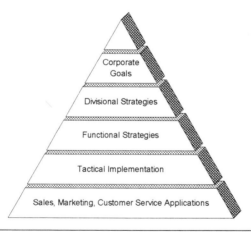

Figure 1.3 Linkage of system capabilities with hierarchy of goals

By linking the ability to execute tactical action more efficiently and effectively, it is possible to associate each capability to tactics and strategies, and finally to corporate goals. Since corporate goals include revenue growth, margin levels, and profitability, a system can be linked to financial success, which forms the basis for justification.

Continuous Improvement

As was described earlier in this chapter, two of the characteristics of the marketplace are the rate of change and the need to deliver value to the customer. These characteristics suggest that the ability to react to change and effectively adapt will be characteristics that define success and perhaps longevity for any organization.

Again, viewing customer responsiveness through the perspective of the sales process, what insights can be gleaned from the systems in place today? Consider the sales process described in figure 1.4.

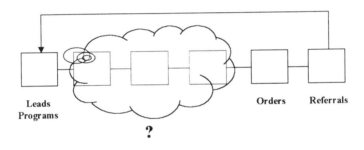

Leads
Programs

Orders   Referrals

?

Figure 1.4 Insight regarding the performance of a typical sales process

Figure 1.4 graphically portrays the significant gulf in information that exists within most organizations. For many organizations, there may not be an accurate count of leads much less information on how many are converted into business and which sources are the most cost effective. Similarly, marketing programs have the same type of blind spot. How well were the programs implemented? What were the customer responses? How much new business did the programs generate?

At the other end of the sales process is the generation of orders. Although these counts are very accurate, the definition of what's working remains an unknown. The same is true of referrals; the system may not even capture the existence of referrals not to mention their source and success in generating new business.

Clearly, the ability to generate better data regarding the progress of sales campaigns should result in improved productivity. This is often a significant component of system justification; however, more importantly is the opportunity to leverage this information to continuously improve the processes. It is difficult to quantify this effect for justification purposes, but strategically, it represents an ability to adapt quickly and effectively to the market. Both of these capabilities are keystones to maintaining competitive advantage.

Chapters 10 and 11 discuss various quality related tools that can be used for monitoring customer centric processes and improving them on a continuous basis. This will not happen unless senior management recognizes the opportunity and dedicates the resources to make it happen. The project team's responsibility is to make this linkage apparent to senior management and the organization at-large.

2

The Value Chain Model

One of the challenges of analyzing sales and customer service requirements is to develop a conceptual framework for the analysis. This chapter provides a conceptual model defined as a *value chain*. The rationale for this model is that organizational needs can be effectively analyzed by understanding how value is delivered to the customer today and how technology can be employed to deliver increased value in the future. This model is useful in providing a strategic context. A second model refered to as a *sales process model* is introduced later in this book. The sales process model provides a more tactical or process level of detail that will be used extensively to position specific areas for justification.

This chapter should be viewed as a strategic overview of the CRM process. It attempts to provide a rationale for applying technology and serves as the conceptual framework for all of the concepts presented.

A Value Chain Perspective

It should be obvious that change is not going to slow down; indeed it is reasonable to expect that change will increase in tempo in the foreseeable future. If strategic management is to be effectively deployed to the operating levels of an organization, then there must be a shift from crisis management to one of opportunity management. The opportunity manager takes the time to solve tomorrow's predictable problems today. In general, planning is concerned with identifying today's decisions that allow for tomorrow's capabilities. What is required is a model that helps the organization to identify opportunities and develop strategies; one such model is referred to as the value chain i.e. how is value created and delivered to the ultimate customer?

The toolbox of the 21st Century is essentially in place today. Unfortunately, capabilities such as e-mail and video conferencing are being used as cost saving devices rather than competitive or opportunity impact solutions. This section will develop the concept of the value chain model as an important element in establishing strategy and positioning the sales function and related technology needs.

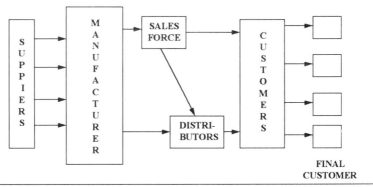

Figure 2.1 The framework for a value chain system

The intent of the value chain is to trace the path of the delivery of products and services to the ultimate customer. It must be emphasized that the model is meant to be conceptual in nature and is not a call to measure costs and time factors to *fourteen decimal places*. The model helps to visualize the conversion, delivery, and communication processes with a focus on the final or end customer.

In the example, the model reflects a manufacturer that sells to a customer base who in turn sells to a final customer. This model is consistent with a consumer goods company, but it is applicable to any business supply entity. The model could reflect the delivery of a service without substantially altering the diagram.

From a value added perspective, the model appears as indicated in figure 2.2.

Figure 2.2 The migration of cumulative value

Each stage is assumed to add value to the process. Note that a corresponding graph could be created for incurred cost at each stage. This perspective would reflect the relative efficiency of each stage. From an opportunity standpoint however, the greatest competitive gain can be achieved by studying the value needs of the final customer. The entire process is meaningless unless the final customer receives commensurate value associated with the purchase. Thus, the strategic need of the manufacturer is to understand the value needs of the final customer and deliver these requirements in a superior manner relative to price so as to achieve competitive advantage.

Value

Central to the concept of the value chain is the definition of value. Although this term is used extensively, it often remains undefined. Intuitively, one would define value, as the price one is willing to pay for the item in question. This is a reasonable definition, but if the issue is broadened to the question of what components or attributes contribute to that perception of value, then the response takes on a different flavor.

Before discussing the question of value attributes, it is important to point out that the term "Final Customer" in the models and discussion is a blanket term used to describe the *customer's customer*. This final customer could be a consumer or another business entity. One should not limit the perspective of this analysis to the next layer of customer on an arbitrary basis. Since the decision regarding the number of layers requires significant discussion, the use of the term, *final customer* will connote a minimum of the next layer.

For business-to-business transactions, the relevant issue of value is "competitiveness" i.e. how does the product or service contribute to the customer's competitive position in the marketplace? Competitiveness can relate to a host of attributes such as cost, flexibility, image, marketing, etc. On this basis, competitiveness is as intangible as value; therefore, an alternative measure is required. A reasonable surrogate for value and competitiveness is profitability. If a supplier helps a customer to be more "profitable," then it is reasonable to assume that the supplier is adding "value." One could argue that cost is an equally appropriate measure, but cost cannot easily accommodate flexibility, time compression, or market related issues that impact a customer's demand. Thus, a supplier's intent should be to positively impact its customers' profitability as effectively as possible, thereby garnering maximum margins for itself.

Given this perspective, it should be obvious why a supplier should be interested in its customers' strategies and customer base. This information will provide insight into capabilities that the customer will value because of the contribution to its competitiveness. Knowledge of the end user base provides a validation of the customer's strategy and expands the supplier's perspective regarding enterprise solutions that dramatically improve delivered value, while increasing margins for the supplier.

The alternative to this approach is to take the **four-wall** mentality that is "what is good for me is good for the customer." This attitude is conducive to thinking **inside the box**. If ever there was an era that requires thinking **outside the box**, it is now. Corporate strategy that is created in the vacuum of the corporation will result in being caught in a no-win competitive corner. Value will be the currency of the 21st Century.

A Process Perspective

Having defined value and the value chain model, it is now possible to discuss the management of this relationship from a process perspective. Most organizations have only a partial view of the value chain as indicated in figure 2.3.

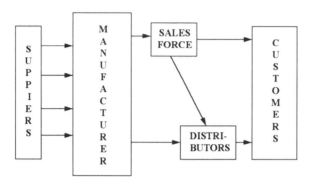

Figure 2.3 Manufacturer's view of value ends with the initial customer

The missing portion of the model is identifying the final customer. Manufacturers do not know their customer's customer and are often ignorant of the customer's competitive strategy. Without these vital pieces of information, it should be clear that the manufacturer would be purely guessing regarding opportunities to add value. Further, the manufacturer has no mechanism to decide whether a specific customer is one that will grow or is worthy of investment in terms of building a closer relationship. These issues are critical to strategy formulation, but also to tactical use of the sales force. In general, one would want to be able to guide the sales force in seeking a customer mix that will match value with price; failure to do this will inevitably erode margins. Assuming that the manufacturer establishes a competitive and value oriented dialog with the customer base, the value model takes on the following form:

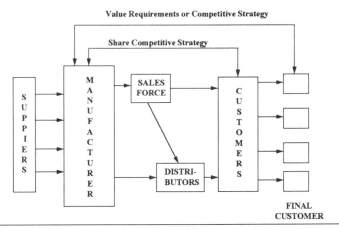

Figure 2.4 Extending the value chain to the ultimate customer

In this diagram, the manufacturer has a dramatically improved perspective regarding opportunities and risk:

- Knowledge of customer strategies and their customer base allows the manufacturer to segment by valueand growth potential rather than simply volume or SIC classification.
- Knowledge of competitive strategy provides insight as to how the manufacturer can increase the customers' profitability e.g. systems that reduce lead-time or inventory requirements.
- Knowledge of competitive strategy provides insight regarding value added by distributors and their relevance to the customer longer term.
- Knowledge of the value needs and direction of the customer's customers provides additional insight regarding competitive opportunities, growth potential, and viability of the customer.

Armed with this type of information the manufacturer will have a better perspective with regards to issues such as:

- The opportunity for joint marketing and which end users to target.
- The impact of shortening order fulfillment and other related transactions.
- Feedback from the customer to guide development efforts.
- Customer impact to identify value added opportunities that the sales force or distributors could fulfill.

- The input to help sharpen customer mix and targeting of sales activity.
- Insight from the customer to identify the relevance of the sales force and/or distributors.

Supply Chain Management

From a technology standpoint, a supply chain can be thought of as an information conduit that balances a company's business needs on both the supply side and demand side. The goal of Supply Chain Management (SCM) is to optimize the business operations of a company so that it can meet customer needs across the supply enterprise, which includes distributors, suppliers, and customers. Graphically, this relationship can be described as follows:

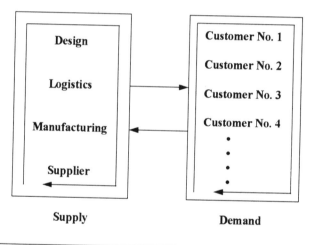

Figure 2. 5 The need to extend supply chain management to the field

It is the intent of supply chain management to reduce the requirement of system level inventories while substantially reducing total cycle times. These goals represent an opportunity to substantially reduce costs, while increasing responsiveness - a major source of competitive advantage.

Although the concept of SCM has been in existence for years, it has become a very "hot topic" as companies seek to reduce cycles times.

Technology has fueled the expansion in interest. Object-oriented programming has made it possible to better integrate the activities and functions on the supply side, whereas the Internet has expanded the ability to link and integrate demand and supply activities. The current toolbox allows for the following types of applications:

- General purpose e-mail
- Dissemination of public and marketing information
- Access to technical specifications
- Sales proposals
- Electronic catalogs
- Shipping status
- Product/service configurators
- Shipping reservation/commitment
- Electronic data interchange
- Financial transactions
- Product data management
- Electronic buying groups

These capabilities provide the framework to interface with customers in radically new ways. The ability to exchange data and information instantaneously, provides an opportunity to create new business rules, which essentially changes the competitive landscape.

These technologies and strategies can have a major impact on the structure of the sales force. The ability of the customer to obtain information directly (electronically) from the corporation means that certain tasks and roles historically assigned to the sales function may be eliminated or accomplished without a direct sales force. This same technology offers opportunity for the direct sales force to add value to the customer. If a company follows a strict cost or productivity approach, it will no doubt seek to reduce the size of the sales force. However, an opportunity-based strategy will seek to gain competitive advantage through adding value. Thus, knowledge of the customer base and its ultimate markets becomes the keystone of addressing this issue. The next section will address this issue in greater detail.

Relevant Technologies

Understanding customer strategies and their target markets is essential to the strategies associated with competition in the next century. Growth strategies are based on innovation and managing customer retention. Global competition is dependent on blending a central strategy with the realities of local markets and knowledge management is focused on customer based solutions.

Customer retention is becoming recognized as a requisite for profitable growth in the next millenium. Recent research has indicated that customer retention and customer satisfaction is not synonymous. A satisfied customer may not be a long-term customer; it is a question of **relevance**. What satisfies the customer today may not be consistent with tomorrow's needs. Thus, understanding customer direction and strategy is no longer a luxury but a necessity.

Based on the clear benefits and imperative of this information, most organizations should be doing this type of analysis. However, gathering this information and analyzing it competes with the immediacy of today's needs. Fortunately, today's toolbox contains a number of technologies that facilitate the process and offer value added that is difficult to emulate without technology. The following examples provide an overview of these capabilities:

- **Web Sites:** A web sites can be used for a variety of value added applications including:
  - ❖ Provide a source of general information to customers and the customer's customer.
  - ❖ Provide a means for end users to communicate to the organization e.g. electronic surveys.
  - ❖ Replace electronic catalogs
  - ❖ Provide design/recommendation capabilities (configurators)
  - ❖ Provide order status for direct ship customers
  - ❖ Provide inventory status and order entry capabilities.
- **The Web as a Network**
  - ❖ Provides an e-mail capability

> ❖ Provides EDI capabilities to a wide range of customers due to cost of setup and operation.

■ **Sales Force Automation:** This technology can provide a diverse set of applications that can add value via the sales force. Examples of these applications include:

> ❖ Opportunity or territory management applications facilitate capturing customer strategies and other value preferences. These applications often facilitate team support of the customer.
>
> ❖ Configurators can be used for order entry, proposals, or the generation of design recommendations.
>
> ❖ Electronic catalogs can provide instant access to reference parts and pricing. This data can include specifications and pricing.
>
> ❖ Multi-media represents an opportunity to graphically demonstrate concepts and communicate with diverse audiences. The technology also augments training and raises overall skill levels.

■ **Call Center Technology:** Call center technology provides an effective interface from inside sales and utilizing customer service for inside sales purposes.

The implications for the value chain model can be characterized as follows:

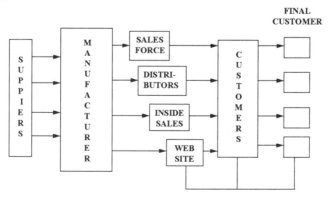

Figure 2.6 An integrated model

Although the model does not appear radically different, the impact
of these technologies can be enormous. Consider the following:

1. The sales interface now consists of four separate entities that
represent dramatically different cost and value added options. The new
mix of capabilities should reduce costs, while providing desirable value
added for the customer. Although the cost aspect is clearly desirable,
the emphasis should be on delivering unique value. For example:

- ❖ The direct sales force could provide tools that help the
  customer reduce market cycle time.
- ❖ Distributors could add services to the value mix by
  providing fabrication or additional design capabilities.
- ❖ An inside sales capability may be desirable for customers
  who desire instantaneous service and sales expertise.
- ❖ A web site may be capable of unique services not addressed
  by the above options; for example, searching for optional
  sources of supply, etc.

Thus, each component provides a basic set of services, but also provides
a unique capability. Each customer receives value added consistent with
their perspective of needs.

2. Each component of the sales effort could provide a unique value add,
while a networked capability would allow for timely communication and
coordination. Thus, customers would receive a service delivery
capability that leverages the best aspects of each component.

3. The web site can be used as a vehicle for communication with
customers and end users. The company can benefit from a better
understanding of the final market, which will guide strategy with its
customer base.

Developing A Strategy

Despite the fact that these technologies can dramatically impact
competitive position, they represent an enormous amount of investment
and organizational change. Thus, implementing this level of change
requires a careful plan and a multi-functional approach. It is beyond the

intent of this white paper to provide a detailed implementation plan; however, the following outline does provide an overall plan of attack:

1. Members of senior management should be utilized to conduct high level meetings with customers that represent the top 80 percent of value (80/20 rule). These meetings should cover specific topics such as competitive strategies, patterns in the market, end user industries, use of technology (particularly EDI and the Web), expectations for suppliers moving into the 21st Century, value provided by the sales force, etc.

2. Members of regional management should conduct parallel high level meetings with customers that represent a sampling of the remainder of the customer base.

3. An internal study should be conducted to determine internal readiness for EDI and Internet capabilities. This study should also capture performance implications such as reduction in head count, cycle time, and operational costs.

4. The various business-briefing teams need to summarize their findings. The findings should be categorized by value needs and strategy versus product considerations. In general, they should address directional issues involving linkage with the company including EDI, Internet, and the direct sales force.

5. Assuming that there is sufficient rationale and concerns on the part of the customer base, a study of EDI and Internet capability should be launched. The intent of the study should be to establish an implementation strategy.

6. On a parallel path, a team should be established to define the needs of the sales organization in terms of system applications. This study should integrate internal needs with external customer expectations and present on implementation strategy similar to item No. 5 above.

7. If the company is not currently using inside sales, it is best to approach this aspect on a limited regional basis. This approach

provides the insight for successful implementation and proves the model and results to justify expansion to other regions.

8. The findings from items 5, 6, and 7 should be integrated into a unified implementation plan with timetables and expected results.

Given this model as a conceptual overview, the next chapter will discuss the historical difficulties with justifying new technology and provide an overview for the rest of the book.

3

The Justification Dilemma

It appears as though the disappointing news regarding sales force automation success is on a constant track. At the 1997 DCI Boston SFA conference, Forrester Report disclosed that only 28 percent of Fortune 1000 companies report highly successful sales automation efforts. These results coincide with other historical studies that have suggested 50+ percent failure rates. Unfortunately, what these reports fail to divulge is the basis for the evaluation. If a project does not have a well-defined and broadly communicated objective, success or failure can depend on whom within the corporation is asked the question. Lack of defined project goals is analogous to the adage "if you don't know where you are going, any road will take you there." The corollary however is that once you arrive, you may not like what you see.

Despite many years of communicating a consistent message to the end user community, end user organizations still tend to search out software solutions before they understand their operational needs. The ultimate result is typically a realization that the true needs of the organization differ from the capabilities of the purchased solution. The answer to this dilemma is the implementation of a comprehensive needs assessment that links CRMS requirements with organizational needs, strategies, and goals. The result of this analysis should include the following topics or documents:

- Strategic Overview: Define how the proposed system will contribute to "mission critical" or essential corporate goals and strategies.
- Implementation Plan: Provides a multi-year (4-5 years) plan that defines all relevant costs and resources required to develop, enhance, and maintain the proposed system.
- Cost Justification (ROI) Analysis: Establish the cause and effect relationships between benefits and investment and present a ROI analysis to support the investment.

When the steps are implemented properly, the organization knows where it is going, why, and what the organization will look like when it gets there. Under these circumstances, one can truly differentiate whether lack of success relates to faulty assumptions, implementation errors, or system performance issues.

Getting to this level of understanding is certainly not simple, but it is essential. This book is primarily focused on the issue of cost justification; by necessity, it will also address issues that would normally be covered in a Strategic Overview document. Consistent with the chronology of a well-defined project, the book follows a track that addresses preliminary planning as well as post implementation review and monitoring of results.

The book is organized in a sequential manner similar to the issues that a project team needs to address in the development of a sales automation initiative. Chapter 4 address the challenges of navigating the various corporate planning processes and ensuring that the project is incorporated into the necessary budgets to ensure proper prioritization.

Consideration of planning processes is often an after-thought and this lack of planning can significantly delay an initiative. In order to assemble the right type of project team, there must be senior level support; therefore, Chapters 5 and 6 emphasize how to tap into senior management concerns and position sales force automation as an essential element of corporate strategy.

Chapters 7-10 identify how to analyze processes and basically what to look for in terms of improvements. Chapter 11 provides an overview of a set of group problem solving and analysis techniques, which should facilitate project team evaluation of organizational performance challenges on a continuous basis.

Chapter 12 provides a guide to identifying the types of costs and investment incurred in the development and maintenance of a sales force automation initiative. This information is essential to the development of an ROI calculation that will protect vital support functions as the project phases into the post implementation period.

Chapters 13-15 address the issues associated with organizing the project team data and assembling a winning project proposal. Chapter 15 provides an example that explains the mechanics of the process and the calculations.

Chapter 17 provides insight regarding the linkage of corporate goals and operational processes. Using cause and effect analysis, the chapter provides a guide relative to how to identify these relationships and how to define metrics that will demonstrate improvement.

Finally, Chapter 18 summarizes the process and provides a wrap-up type of perspective. It is very difficult to separate the elements of a comprehensive needs assessment from those that specifically address the issues of justification. There are several texts available that address the issues associated with a needs assessment; these are included in the bibliography.

4

Planning Processes and Budgets

Sales force automation involves a significant outlay of funds and commits the organization to an on-going stream of expenses to support the system into the future. Corporations plan for these types of programs using standard planning processes and budgets. It is through this mechanism that organizations control anticipated future spending and forecast profitability requirements. As a general rule of thumb, if the initiative is not in the budget, it is not going to happen during that budget period. In the short term, however, it is often possible to shift funding between accounts thereby permitting some investment in the project. But in the context of total project funding, the initiative must be budgeted and approved.

Key Planning Processes

Typically, there are four types of planning processes that operate within most corporations. Although they may be called different names (officially and unofficially), the four processes include the following:

1. **Annual Plan:** The annual plan comprehends the projected revenue, margins, and expenses anticipated during the fiscal year. This plan is often created during the last quarter of the preceding fiscal year so that budgets and goals are established before the beginning of the next fiscal year.

2. **The Marketing Plan:** This plan is also a one-year plan but often it has a different time horizon than the Annual Plan. The reason for this difference is that the Marketing Plan contains commitments to programs or media events that will occur during the Annual Plan. In general, this plan will include advertising, promotions, collateral, lead management, and perhaps training budgets for the up-coming

year. This is an important plan to be familiar with because major dollar levels are often associated with this budget.

3. **The Capital Plan:** This plan pertains to all capital purchases or project initiatives that will occur in the upcoming fiscal year. Since it is project or major purchase oriented, the plan is often created before the Annual Plan. There are often two acceptances or approval levels in the Capital Plan process, the first approval level is to get your project level included in the budget and the second level is to get it approved for startup in the next fiscal year. Thus, just getting the project included in the Capital Plan does not automatically result in having the funding available for the next year.

4. **The long-range or Strategic Plan:** This plan often covers a period of three to five years. It is similar to the Annual Plan in that it contains revenue, margins, and expense projections; however, more importantly, it should contain references to risk and strategies that the company is considering regarding the performance levels reflected in the plan.

Leveraging The Planning Processes

Knowledge of the timing and content of these formal planning processes is essential to any CRM initiative. If you are unfamiliar with these processes, it is essential that you become knowledgeable or find someone who is willing to guide you in these matters. The timing implications are portrayed in Figure 3.1. Note that missing input into a planning cycle could delay a project by as much as a year.

The plan, which will have the most profound implications on the ability to implement a CRM initiative, is the Capital Budget. A typical CRM project includes significant capital (depreciable assets) investment as well as many expense related expenditures. For this reason, the CRM project must be included in the Capital Plan, it receives visibility that it is a future event and it receives a preliminary OK as a priority initiative. When the time comes to actually start the project (design phase) a formal project proposal is submitted to the Board of Directors. Given that this item was included in the capital budget usually means that the initiative has a good chance for approval. However, consider going to the Board for authorization for a project that is super important but wasn't thought of when the capital plan was assembled. Which situation would you rather be in? The Capital Budget tends to be a showstopper from a funding perspective. Since CRM requires capital funds, the money must come from this source (there is limited ability to swap out budgets).

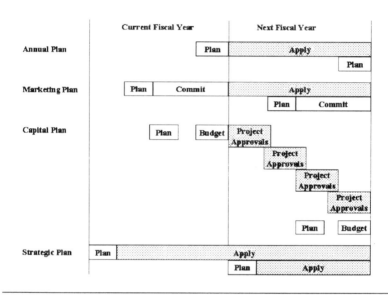

Figure No. 4.1 Calendar relationship among the planning processes

In the short term, the Annual and Marketing Plans can be very important. For immediate expense items, it may be possible to shift expense items amongst line items. Using this flexibility, one may be able to fund studies or gain resources to assemble a budget estimate for the initiative and conduct needs assessment activities. It may also be possible to do some design work including a prototype but beyond these activities, the project requires capital or project approval.

The Annual and Marketing Plans are also important as a means of benchmarking current levels of expenditure. As will be discussed in subsequent chapters, cost reduction can represent an important element of a system justification. On the other side of the investment equation, support requirements for the system may mean incremental head count or new line items on the budget. In these circumstances, it is important to ensure that these additions are incorporated into the planning process so that the resultant budgets contain the necessary resources. The alternative to not gaining the budget commitment is either a diluted solution and/or diluted services. Either of these results can severely compromise or otherwise doom an initiative to failure.

Lastly, the Strategic or Business Plan represents an important source of information regarding strategies and risks the company faces in the future. Obviously, if CRM potentially leverages some of these strategies, then this is an important element of the justification and that linkage needs to be reflected in future versions of the Strategic Plan. If there is no direct linkage with these strategies, then the strategic plan needs to reflect how the initiative will help the company achieve the growth and profitability projections included in the plan. By using this type of visibility, senior management will be reminded of the strategic significance of CRM.

Figure 4.2 is provided to indicate the relationship of the planning processes relative to a CRM implementation.

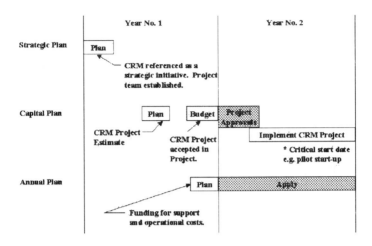

Figure 4.2 CRM Project timing relative to planning schedules

Note that in the example provided in Figure 4.2, it is possible to work backward from a critical start date, such as the beginning of a pilot, and identify when planning needs to start.

5

Strategic Initiatives and Gap Analysis

The justification of a CRM system is based on future performance. Therefore, the foundations for the analysis are the organization's assumptions regarding future performance and the planned strategies to achieve that performance. Gap analysis is a technique for projecting expected versus desired performance levels. Senior management is vitally interested in achieving long term performance goals and closing the gap between expected and actual performance.

Recognizing senior management's interest in this area of performance and the fact that CRM can leverage the impact of strategic initiatives thereby reducing or eliminating potential gap, CRM justification must consider these initiatives. This chapter provides an overview of how to identify areas of gap and the role of CRM in leveraging common strategic initiatives.

Identifying The Gaps

For many organizations, the challenges associated with future performance can be summarized as a series of corporate quadrant charts. For example, the components of sales revenue ($ X 1,000,000 could be described in figure 5.1.

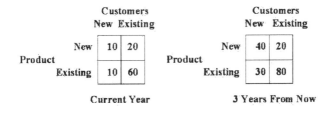

Figure 5.1 Identifying the components of growth

In this example, current revenue is $100 million (10+20+10+60) versus $170 million (40+20+30+80). This corresponds to a 20 percent growth rate. Note that the growth for revenue from existing customers is $70 million (current) versus $110 million (projected) or approximately a 16 percent growth rate. The growth for revenue from new customers is $30 million (current) versus $60 million (projected) this corresponds to a growth rate of over 25 percent. What if the company has had problems acquiring new customers or selling the new products? Clearly, the company will be in jeopardy under these conditions.

This type of risk can be described as a potential gap between the desired target versus the current projection.

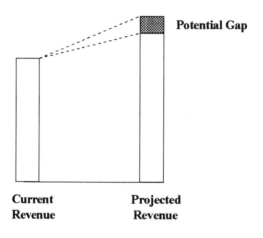

Figure 5.2 Identifying performance gaps

The relevance for a CRM system is that if senior management views the initiative as helping to fill that gap, they will be highly supportive of the initiative.

Identifying Key Strategies

In addition, senior management is very likely to have articulated one or more strategies that are designed to keep the organization competitive.

It is not possible to create a comprehensive view of all these initiatives, but the following items will provide a basis for discussion.

1. **Decentralization:** Decentralization is a management philosophy that is based on driving decisions down to the lowest level possible. The rationale for decentralization is to improve accountability and the quality of decision making. This type of strategy is appropriate where local pricing and/or promotional activity is key to success. The success of such a strategy is tied to the quality of the tools provided to management. Quality decisions should drive better utilization of resources; thus, CRM can be employed to provide better information and appropriate decision making tools. In this scenario, it would be appropriate (as an example) to claim future increases in promotional productivity due to the SFA initiative. M&M/Mars implemented a sales force automation initiative to support a need to move decision making regarding staffing and promotion management to field sales management. Justification for the system included productivity gains that were tied to improved decision making.

2. **Partnering:** A partnering strategy calls for tight integration with customers. This often involves team selling and coordination. Both of these capabilities are tied to CRM therefore, incremental revenue associated with this strategy could be considered.

3. **Acquisitions/Divestiture:** If the company is planning to use acquisitions as a mechanism to accelerate growth and the company desires to absorb these companies into one structure, clearly this calls for a CRM solution. CRM can help reps learn new product lines and support them while taking on new customers. In this case, CRM could be associated with cost avoidance associated with a much slower integration of the sales forces. Ciba Geigy implemented sales force automation as a result of a need to combine the merger of the Ciba and Geigy companies into one sales force. The justification was based on higher productivity and better penetration of the market.

If the sales forces are not intended to be merged, the relevant issue will be one of coordination. Is it likely that the two sales forces will be calling on the same customer or will there be opportunities for cross selling? Coordination of this type can best be supported by technology; therefore, incremental revenue attributable to such activity could be directly linked to CRM.

4. **Customer Retention:** Retention is really the result of a comprehensive program of improving service and the quality of the interface with customers. The financial impact of this type of strategy far exceeds the traditional marketing cost differentiation of 5-10 times the sales and marketing cost to close a gain a new customer.

    As figure 5.3 indicates, the value of a customer increases over time. Revenue increases as the customer grows and as the supplier's share of the customer grows. Cost savings increase as the organization learns how to meet the customer's needs efficiently. Satisfied customers serve as effective references and pass on referrals. Long term customers also tend to be less price sensitive; thus, margins are maintained or perhaps increase. Overall, the total effect of these factors far exceeds the original acquisition cost.

    If your company has defined customer retention as a strategic initiative, then you need to determine whether this decision is based on an analysis or on the basis of a perceived trend. It is doubtful that a company can be seriously committed to a retention strategy if it has not analyzed the financial impact of customer retention using it's own data. The reason for this vulnerability is the commitment to change and analysis associated with a retention strategy. Without a firm conviction that the effort will pay significant returns, the strategy will falter.

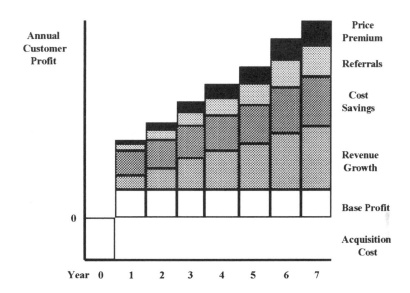

Figure 5.3 The economics of customer retention[3]

If the strategy is based on specific estimates for your company, then you have to find out who is the keeper of the data. The next question is, what are the roles of the sales organization and customer service in the customer retention strategy? What specific tasks (processes) are involved? What are the expectations regarding time commitments, quality of work, reporting and skill sets? These areas become sources of cost reduction and profit improvement. The organization must assess how well these functions can accomplish these tasks with today's capabilities? What is the return associated with strengthening these capabilities?

5. **New Product Introductions:** Most product-oriented companies are experiencing ever shortening product life cycles. This means more new product introductions and typically, success is measured in

---

[3] Reichheld, Frederick F. *The Loyalty Effect*, Boston: Harvard Business School Press, 1996.

terms of rate of penetration in the market place. Clearly, if the life cycle is shortened, then the profitability of the product over its life will be highly correlated to how rapidly it is accepted in the marketplace. These requirements place considerable reliance on the sales force, which must learn how to sell the new items, and productively target the right prospects. In its current state, the sales force may not have the capacity to learn the new products at the necessary rate of introduction into the market place and there may be insufficient time to sell-in new products while maintaining the existing requirements. Further, the sales force may lack effective qualifying and/or targeting tools to execute the strategy. The alternatives are definitely limited, either the company must add people or the methods it uses for product introductions must be changed.

6. **Value Based Strategies:** These types of strategies are typically oriented at maintaining margins and/or improving customer retention. A value-based strategy is built on the premise of helping the customer improve their profitability (business to business model). Inevitably, the strategy embraces both product and services. For the sales force, the strategy means that the sales rep must be able to make these differences real and relevant to the procurement community. Further, the sales rep must be able to review performance statistics with the customer to ensure that the customer recognizes "value received." What are the skill and knowledge base required making this happen? Can the sales organization do it? At what cost?

7. **Structural Strategies:** Organizational strategies can take on many forms. For example, creation of a national account group, separation of sales effort by business unit, consolidation of sales effort, introduction of new channels of distribution, are all structural strategies. Challenges associated with structural strategies include coordination, communication, training, and cross selling. There is typically a learning curve and without proper tools, the result may be a set of new problems that eclipse the old ones. Sales force

automation can often provide the infrastructure required to be successful.

Establishing the Base Line

In order to demonstrate the benefits of sales force automation, there must be a base line of comparison. During the previous chapters, it has been emphasized that the source of the base line information is often resident within the long range or strategic plan. If this type of documentation does not exist, then you must seek out some reasonable assumptions regarding revenue growth, margins, sales costs, and overall profitability. This type of information can be gleaned from marketing and the CFO.

At the most basic level, the data will include the following types of performance criteria:
- Revenue will grow at a compound rate of 10 percent per year.
- Margins will remain at 30 percent.
- Sales costs will remain at 7 percent of revenue.
- Marketing costs will grow at a rate of 8 percent per year.
- Profitability will increase at a rate of 12 percent per year.

In addition, it is critical to capture the assumptions associated with the numbers. For example, rates of product introduction, inflation, key initiatives, acquisitions, etc. This body of information forms the basis for a non-automation or no-change in automation (if you have a system) scenario.

6

Senior Management Perspective

Focus On The Numbers

Senior management has a wide range of responsibilities and concerns ranging from the market place to management succession and the value of the stock. However, most senior managers are vitally interested in the *numbers*. Although the format of the numbers may differ somewhat by organization, they typically revolve around revenue, margins, profitability, and return on assets (ROA). Very often, senior management bonus structures are built on this same set of figures.

This does not mean that senior management is disinterested in the strategic importance of initiatives such as CRM, surely the appreciation is present. In balance, however, an initiative that can be linked to one or more of these measures will surely be prioritized over one that does not have such linkage.

Within CRM, the linkage with these factors takes on the following characteristics:

1. **Revenue:** Increases are typically due to changes in sales rep productivity (Revenue/sales rep or sales costs).

2. **Margins:** Increase through better customer targeting, product/services mix, or by adding value to the customer in a way that leverages margin.

3. **Profitability:** Increased profitability is often achieved by avoiding or reducing costs.

4. **Return on Assets (ROA):** Since CRM typically adds to the asset base, increasing ROA is typically achieved through a disproportionate increase in revenue or through decreased asset requirements such as inventory or offices.

The Value of Bellwether Numbers

Despite the power and importance of these *numbers,* most senior managers recognize that they represent a forensic (after the fact) view of the world and therefore have limited value in managing the *now* situation. Most organizations have very few early warning systems that indicate difficulty for the future. Thus, if CRM can be used to generate this type of early warning, then it would represent a capability with significant strategic value. Chapter 17 discusses and describes the linkage of sales related performance metric to organizational financial goals. These metrics are referred to as drivers in that they tend to drive financial results. By studying the drivers, it should be possible to demonstrate bellwether characteristics.

Related to early warning is the issue of risk. Senior management is well aware of the forces that influence ultimate success. If a CRM initiative can be shown to reduce the risk of not meeting certain numbers, then again, it will be viewed as having significant strategic value.

7

Sales Performance Data

What Data Is Available Today

Justification of a CRM system is often hampered by the lack of appropriate performance measures that one could use to estimate the impact of automation and later validate that the estimate was indeed correct. Since most sales forces have accounting systems and systems for tracking incentive performance, it is fairly common to have access to the following types of data:

- Revenue growth rate
- Revenue per sales rep
- Revenue per sales and marketing head count
- Cost of sales/marketing as a percentage of revenue
- Average margins
- Total number of sales people versus authorized head count
- Average number of accounts per rep
- Average revenue per account
- Number of accounts accounting for 80 percent of revenue
- Average cycle time from receipt of order to shipment
- Average line items and dollars associated with each order
- Percent of sales reps meeting or exceeding quota

What Data Does The Organization Need?

At the account level, most organizations do not have a handle on the following:

- Account profitability
- Customer retention
- Lead management success rates
- Win/loss ratios and reasons for losing
- Sales funnel statistics
- Share of customer (share of potential business)

- Which accounts make up 80 to 90 percent of revenue, profit?
- What end markets do the customers serve?
- Parent - offspring relationships (who owns whom?)
- Customer acquisitions
- Returns or other discrepancies
- On-time delivery of product (customer's perspective)

Without this type of information, it is pretty difficult to assess whether you are doing business with the right customers and whether you are winning the battle for a fair share of their business.

Utilization of Time

At the sales rep level, it is difficult to determine what portion of their day is spent on selling activities and whether that time is spent with the right prospects, customers, and opportunities. Thus, at a minimum, one would need to know:
- Time spent on proactive sales tasks
- Time spent resolving problems
- Travel time
- Coverage

Even these figures fail to ascertain whether the sales rep is leveraging available time, it does however indicate trends in availability.

Opportunity Management

Opportunity management perhaps offers the greatest potential for improving insight relative to process performance. Consider the generic model provided in figure 6.1

Figure 7.1 Generic opportunity management phases.

Typical opportunity management statistics include the following:

- Average overall cycle time for this process
- Total number of opportunities processed
- Percent opportunities closed
- Win/loss analysis (when we win why? And when we lose why?)
- Cycle time for key support sub-processes; for example, proposal generation, literature fulfillment, contract generation, and response to original inquiry.
- Average sales rep hours spent on each phase of the opportunity
- Average cycle time spent in each phase
- Disqualification or loss rate per opportunity stage

If these figures are not currently available within the organization, then base line figures need to be established. This can be accomplished through surveys or interviews. Field management must then do an assessment of the degree to which these figures could be improved if they were available on a timely basis. The estimates form the foundation for projecting improvements in sales productivity.

In general, one would want to collapse the overall cycle time and to minimize time spent on opportunities that will not be closed in the relevant future. Measuring cycle times and the quantity of opportunities processed through each phase provides valuable insight regarding overall performance and impediments to improvement.

Lead Management

Similar to opportunity management is lead management; in fact, a lead may be a specific opportunity. Lead management however, has characteristics that are unique; therefore they are best described separately. The generation of leads is an expensive process involving advertising, referrals, direct mail, and trade shows. Once a lead is received, it is often qualified by telephone and/or other checks before forwarding to the field (literature fulfillment?) Inadequately qualified leads waste field resource time and can delay response to higher value leads. Given the costs and implications of a viable lead generation system, it is crucial to understand the relative effectiveness of both the lead generation sources and the qualification steps used prior to release

to the field. Bearing these issues in mind, the following statistics are appropriate:
- The number of leads generated by source
- Cost per lead
- The percent of leads that generate business within a specific time period (by source)
- The cycle time between receipt of the lead at the source to a physical call by a field rep
- The percentage of leads reaching the field sales reps that generate business within a specific period of time (by source or qualifying agent).

Managing Improvement

There is a commonly accepted management concept that you can only mange what can be measured. Most sales organizations are starved for information. The reason for this is that sales process related data is not captured by other formal systems. With the exception of order entry and distribution, the field must gather its own information. Thus, a CRM system can provide much needed insight regarding what is happening within the sales process and within the market. Although control should not be the focus for sales automation, it should be clear to management that the system provides information and reporting capabilities that are impractical given the existing infrastructure.

8

Time Allocation

Perhaps one of the most confusing and overemphasized aspects of justification is related to face time and converting lost time into face time, which will hopefully generate more sales. Certainly, the appeal to increase face time is logical and desirable but it may not be reflected in reality. To explore these ideas further, consider the following discussion.

Establishing Face Time

There are a number of ways that overall time allocation can be established, these include:

1. **Stop Watch:** Sales people are studied as they conduct their business. The resultant numbers are highly accurate in terms of defining the typical time required to accomplish certain common activities but may not reflect actual behavior.

2. **Work Sampling:** This approach is a statistical technique that asks reps to record their activity by classification at random times during the day. This data can be accumulated over time and provides statistically accurate measures of how much time is spent in various types of activities. The validity of this data of course is dependent on the accuracy of reporting by the reps. The data is further limited by the fact that the time allocation cannot be evaluated by examining the methods and behavior exhibited by the sales reps (this is a disadvantage over the stop watch approach).

3. **Survey:** As the name implies, surveys involve sending questionnaires to the field that provide input relative to attitudes and practices. The questions can include allocation or utilization of

time. This approach is less scientific than work sampling but it requires less time and cost to apply.

4. **Interviews:** Similar to survey results, one-on-one and group interviews can be used to generate a profile of a typical sales rep by asking questions related to how much of their day (percentage basis) is spent in certain activities.

Obviously, the results of techniques 2-4 have more relevance to activities that represent 10 percent or more of total time because unless activities occur on a regular basis, it is difficult to estimate their impact below this level. Techniques 1 and 2 are more invasive, but they represent more accurate data from a statistical perspective.

Defining The Total Day

Another critical issue has to do with the boundaries of the time under consideration. Is the perspective limited to the forty hour workweek or should the perspective include time after hours and weekends? Each company must arrive at its own conclusions but an accurate assessment of the true impact of CRM requires a consideration of total work time. A reduction in task time associated with activities that are normally done "after hours" will not increase *face time*. If the focus is on total work time, then techniques such as stop watch and work sampling are not appropriate outside normal working hours. As an example, consider a sales rep that works fifty hours during the week plus five hours every weekend. This results in the general model provided in figure 8.1.

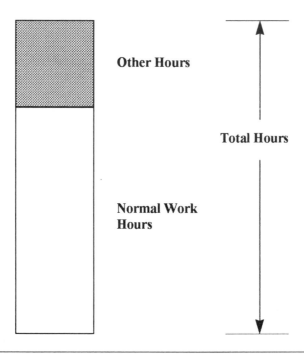

Figure 8.1 Defining the boundaries of total time

If one considers **total** hours to be available (**normal** plus **other**) hours; then, any reduction in required task time could be converted into other productive activity. However, this assumes that the sales rep will increase work load to compensate for any reduction in requirements; this is a tenuous assumption in this era of emphasis on life style. Improvements in face time are more likely to be derived by reducing non-selling activity that occurs during **normal** work hours.

The next logical topic for discussion is the categories to use in capturing utilization of time. Again, stopwatch analysis and work sampling have fewer limitations in terms of the granularity of categories, but using interviews and surveys, the categories need to be broad. The following categories provide some guidance in this area:

1. **Time with customer:** Typically, this is interpreted as within the four walls of the customer's location. Therefore, face to face time is

something less than this percentage. A sub-question to this estimate is what portion of this time is waiting time? Another sub-question relates to time spent with the customer resolving problems associated with orders, deliveries, invoices, etc. For example, 30 percent of the time could be spent in the customer's location but waiting represents 20 percent and 30 percent is spent in problem solving, this leaves only 15 percent in face-to-face selling time.

2. **Phone Time with Customers:** This question raises the question of effective use of the phone to handle customer needs and coverage. The same sub-question can be asked regarding problem resolution.

3. **Travel time:** This should include travel to and from home.

4. **Meetings:** A percentage can often be derived for this category on the basis of so many meetings per month etc.

5. **Training:** Estimating the typical number of days in training divided by the total days worked can derive a percentage.

6. **Phone time with staff:** This should include all telephone time with corporate and regional staff. Sub-questions should include most common topics and time allocations, for example, problem solving, and determining order status information.

7. **Administrative:** This category includes all other tasks. Some of these tasks may be non-selling e.g. expense reports while other may tie directly to sales activities such as proposal generation. Estimates may be appropriate of these sub-activities, if they represent significant portions of the total.

Calculation of Days Worked

An essential part of understanding the time estimates is to determine the average or representative days worked by the typical sales rep. A starting place for this calculation is to assume that there are 22.5 working days per month or 270 days available. Subtract from this number the average vacation days e.g. 10 and the standard holidays e.g. 10 resulting in 250 working days.

Time Allocation: An Example

Using the illustration provided in figure 8.1, assume that the typical sales rep works 55 hours per week and that there are 250 net working days in the year. Then the estimated percentages will generate the hours as indicated in the table.

Category	Estimated %	Assumption	Average Hours
Time w/ Customer	25.0		62.5
Phone time w/ Customer	10.0		25.0
Travel	30.0		75.0
Meetings	.7	One day per month	2.0
Training	1.5	One week per year	4.0
Phone time w/ staff	15.0		37.5
Administrative	17.8		44.0
Totals	100.0		250.0

In this example, travel time, phone time with staff, phone time with customers, and administrative activities represent over 70 percent of total time. Travel time and phone time with staff probably have a major portion of their occurrence during normal working hours; then, improvements in productivity in these areas are more likely to increase face time.

9

The Sales Process

A Generic Model

The sales process represents the heart of any CRM system and should be the center of the justification focus. This chapter will develop the basic mechanics of the sales process and the economics of leveraging the process. Chapter 10 will develop these concepts further by emphasizing the sub-processes that support the sales process.

Although the names and the details are often quite different, most sales processes can be described as follows:

Figure 9.1 A generic sales process

Using this perspective, the steps could represent a territory view, an account view, or some combination of the two. In this context, there is considerable activity in the post-sales phase and beyond. These are the elements that contribute to customer retention.

Opportunity management, on the other hand, tends to be focused at the "deal" level and emphasizes the pre-sales and sales, steps of the process. Typically, these two steps are expanded into five to seven with corresponding definitions and criteria as described in figure 9.2.

Figure 9.2 A generic opportunity management process

A well-coordinated territory strategy would include account strategies for larger accounts, which would influence what *deals* to go after, and how to go after them. A less disciplined approach follows a *numbers* rationale that simply treats each opportunity the same and assumes that the laws of probability will generate results.

Territory Planning

At the territory level, the *Plan* stage should include issues such as deployment and coverage. Deployment is the mechanism by which territories are assigned or balanced. The accuracy or relevance of this mechanism to customer requirements and economics will dictate how effectively this tool works for the organization. For example, if deployment were based on the volume of revenue the account does with the company, one would obviously spend more time with that account, but is it too much or too little? Some accounts want to see less of the sales rep unless a specific need arises. What does the company wish to accomplish with the account? These are just a few of the questions that arise when considering deployment and yet many companies have rudimentary, at best, techniques for planning deployment. The deployment issue does not change face time but it does radically impact the focus and productivity of that time.

Related to deployment is the issue of coverage i.e. how often does the sales rep call on the account and is it a face-to-face call? Deployment and coverage can strongly impact travel time because a poorly conceived deployment/coverage plan can introduce extended drive times and insufficient concentration of calls to balance against the drive time.

Pre-sale and Sell Phase

Depending of the type of product sold and the overall sales cycle time (qualify to close), companies will create multi-stage opportunity management processes that help the organization manage the pre-sale/sell phases.

Frequently, the stages of the opportunity process are described in great detail and this is necessary to maintain the disciplines of describing the state of any given opportunity. However, without automation, it is often difficult to gain accurate data regarding the true number of opportunities and where they are lost or disqualified. For example, an opportunity management process could have the characteristics as provided in figure 9.3.

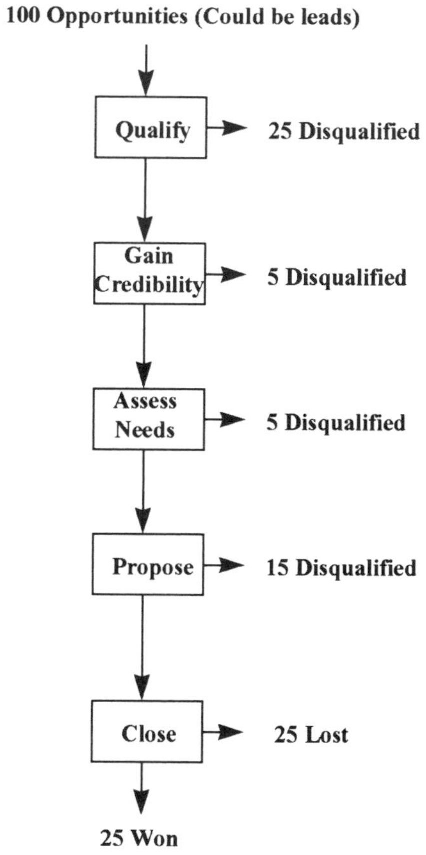

100 Opportunities (Could be leads)

```
        |
     [Qualify]  ➔  25 Disqualified
        |
   [Gain Credibility]  ➔  5 Disqualified
        |
   [Assess Needs]  ➔  5 Disqualified
        |
     [Propose]  ➔  15 Disqualified
        |
      [Close]  ➔  25 Lost
        |
     25 Won
```

Figure 9.3 Yield analysis for a generic opportunity management process

With a 50/50 close ratio, 100 opportunities yields 25 deals. This may not be a bad success ratio for some industries but overall it represents a very inefficient process. Note that an equal number of opportunities are disqualified or lost in the first three steps as opposed to the last two. If the time commitment increased linearly as an opportunity is processed through the steps, then the cumulative time is graphically represented in figure 9.4.

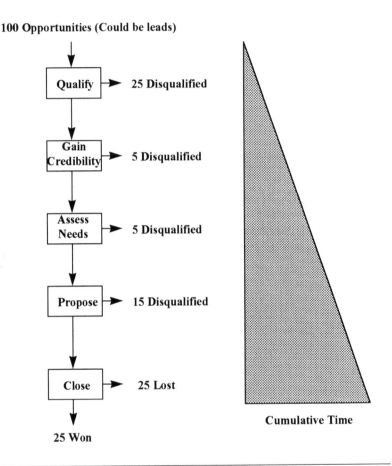

Figure 9.4 Cumulative time investment

Clearly, a more efficient process would involve more stringent qualifying criteria or more effective competitive strategies so that the number processed through the steps is very close to the number of deals

won. Compare the statistics from figure 9.4 and with those from figure
9.5.

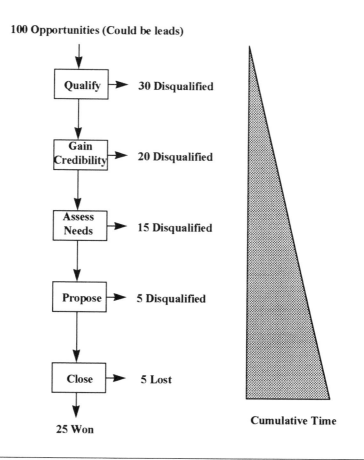

Figure 9.5 Improved qualifying techniques.

In this case sixty-five percent of the applications are disqualified by
the end of Stage No. 3. This allows the rep to spend more effort on
fewer opportunities or to expand the territory to include more
opportunities. The amount of selling time remains constant; it is now
leveraged to create more revenue per the same level of input.

This type of analysis is rather self-evident when the statistics are
disclosed but for most organizations, most of these numbers are

unknowns. Therefore, the process is largely unmanageable. The total number of opportunities or leads are unknown and certainly the qualify rate would be a mystery without some type of automated tracking mechanism. The reasons for won/lost may not be tracked; thus, the organization lacks the ability to take corrective action. All of these statistics represent major productivity blind spots.

Post Sale, Relationship, and Review Stages

The post sale portion of the process addresses everything from order entry through payment for goods and services received. During this stage, the sales rep must deliver precise information to the organization regarding what the customer wants. After the order is entered, the sales rep becomes completely dependent on his organization to deliver against these promises and to keep the sales rep informed of all problems that could impact the customer. In reality, this stage can be a sinkhole for both sales reps and the organization at-large. Frequent incidence of incorrect orders typically result in checks and re-checks inside the organization. These steps slow down delivery processes and tie up sales reps and staff in endless corrective action. In addition, once the order is accepted, sales reps must check with customer service to determine the status of their orders. This contact with customer service consumes sales time and customer service time.

Elimination of order entry errors and the provision of order status reports to the field, through the use of CRM virtually eliminates voice to voice dependence as described above. If your company is bogged down in this type of inter dependence – sales force automation can have a dramatic impact on cost and cycle time associated with order fulfillment.

Building relationships with customers is often defined by many organizations as key to expanding share volume with customers and adding value (which means protecting or improving margins). Unfortunately, this stage of the process is most often neglected in terms of providing sales tools that will assist the sales rep in networking (access to higher levels of management) and providing useful information or insights to the customer. Thus, improving or strengthening this stage requires both defining the required tools and then examining the potential for automating them. The challenge of justifying these tools is that relationship building is an investment in the account. It is difficult to predict the result and the benefit tends to be deferred so that cause and effect are difficult to identify. Thus, projecting improvements in this phase are difficult to prove. However, if your company is committed to customer retention, then CRM applications that strengthen this stage of the sales process must be viewed as contributing to the projected results of the strategy.

The review stage of the process represents an opportunity to share a perspective with the customer relative to current business, future levels of business, and the opportunity to gain more of the customer's business. For organizations that are selling on the basis of price, this review may be an opportunity to thank the customer for the business. However, for organizations that are selling on the basis of value, the review is an opportunity to reinforce, in the customer's mind, the impact of that value. This is often accomplished by a *proof of value* presentation. Strategically, these presentations can have enormous value to the supplier. First, the presentation reinforces in the customer's mind, the value that has been received and it should invite an expansion of the business. If the customer does not agree with the description of the value received, then it is an opportunity to better understand the customer's needs and serve them. The presentation is also an opportunity to gain insight regarding the customer's future direction, this is vital to retaining the customer.

Conducting an effective review requires data and presentation tools that help the sales rep communicate the impact of value received. There is also the issue of capturing customer feedback so that the rep and the organization at-large can utilize this input. This type of information can be vital to customer satisfaction and retention strategies and to gaining a higher share of each customer's business. To project the financial impact, one would have to understand the dollar impact of customer satisfaction and retention and then extrapolate to the improvement offered by automation.

10

Process Analysis

Identifying Sub-Processes

In Chapter 9 the concept of the Sales Process was introduced. It was pointed out that although the steps and measures might be different by company, most processes follow a common model as provided in figure 10.1.

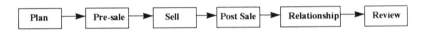

Figure 10.1 A generic sales process

Each stage of the sales process should result in a specific outcome that is unique to that stage. For example, the outcome of the Plan stage may be a territory plan with a set of quantifiable goals. The Pre-Sale outcome could be a customer based needs assessment. The outcome for the Sell stage is typically a purchase order or contract. The Post Sale outcome could be a customer acceptance of an installed product. The relationship phase may have outcomes relating to access to a certain decision-maker or presenting a high level demonstration of capabilities. Finally, the Review stage outcome could be an invitation to study other opportunities for improvement or expand the share of the customer's business. This stage-outcome relationship is summarized in figure 10.2.

A number of steps (or tasks) can be associated with each stage that take the sales process through to the desired outcome or otherwise tells the sales person to re-prioritize the effort (qualification). These steps can be assembled into a logical order referred to as *best practices*

Figure 10.2 Sales process model with stage outcomes

For example, suppose Stage No. 4 is the sell stage for a sales force and that the stage consists of proposing, negotiating, and closing the deal. The outcome is a signed order and the best practice steps might be as follows:

1.0 Develop and present the proposal
- Identify the scope of the opportunity
- Obtain approval for pricing and terms
- Confirm product availability
- Complete cost/benefit justification
- Establish boundaries for negotiation
- Anticipate competitive strategy

2.0 Negotiation
- Update market information
- Negotiate and modify price within boundaries

3.0 Close
- Ask for the order
- Confirm pricing, terms, and delivery schedule
- Develop implementation plan
- Thank the customer

Simply defining these best practices and using them for training and coaching can have a dramatic impact on sales performance. However, automation can enhance this effort further by reinforcing the methodology and reducing the time or skills required to accomplish the tasks.

Having completed the definition of best practices, one can estimate (focus group) the perceived time that the sales force spends on these stages today versus the time that should be spent using best practices. Also, estimates can be derived relative to improvements in yield (revenue/sales rep, calls to close, size of the orders closed, etc.). This represents a first level of improvement.

The second level of improvement is derived by examining the sub-processes that support the best practices for each stage, plus those sub-processes that are not specific to a stage. Figure 10.3 provides an example of typical sub-processes.

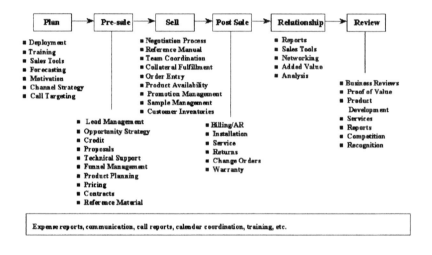

Figure 10.3 Sales process with associated sub-processes

Based on this graphical representation, one can reasonably extrapolate that improving the sub-processes associated with each step will leverage sales rep time utilization and effectiveness, internal resource requirements, and customer responsiveness; whereas, improving the processes below the process boxes will largely impact sales rep time and internal resources. From a cost standpoint, all processes have equal footing; however, those associated with the stages, offer the potential to reduce cost and leverage revenue and margins through an improved customer interface.

Since there are likely to be many processes involved, some type of prioritization is required. One approach is to start with a gap analysis, on a scale of one to five (where five is excellent), rank each sub-process. The next step might be to rank each sub-process as a time sink for the sales force and the organization at-large. This can be done with an A, B, C concept, where A is a major time-sink and C is a minor time sink. Finally, one would want to consider the leverage effect on sales; does this improvement process have a high leverage, H, or low leverage, L. Putting these concepts together, one would have a list as provided below:

Sub-Process	Gap	Sales Time	Internal Resources	Sales Leverage
A	4	C	B	L
B	3	C	A	L
C	2	B	B	H
D	3	A	A	L
E	1	A	B	H
F	4	C	C	H

In this example, sub-processes C and E standout because they are currently not being performed well and they have a high leverage effect on sales. Sub-process D also stands out due to the due to the resources associated with it. Thus, these three sub-processes would be prioritized for analysis.

Process Analysis

There are many techniques for analyzing processes. These range from "back of the envelope" drawings to sophisticated reengineering computer software. Most techniques involve a flow-charting format using different geometric shapes to connote operations, decisions, delays, etc. Common use of symbols include the following:

Inbound goods could be inbound material or a document.

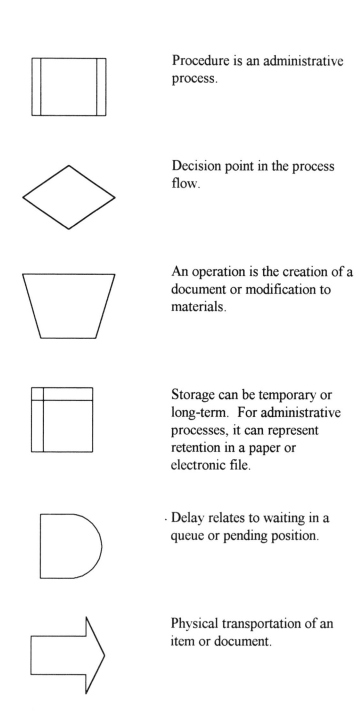

Procedure is an administrative process.

Decision point in the process flow.

An operation is the creation of a document or modification to materials.

Storage can be temporary or long-term. For administrative processes, it can represent retention in a paper or electronic file.

· Delay relates to waiting in a queue or pending position.

Physical transportation of an item or document.

It should be mentioned that there are various coding systems and other symbols that are used, the above are provided as a means for illustration.

As an example, consider a price deviation approval process:

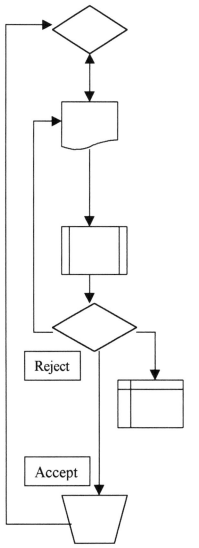

1. The process starts by a customer requesting a more aggressive discount and the sales rep accepts it as a legitimate request.

2. Based on an established procedure, the sales rep completes a price exception request form and forwards the form to a review committee.

3. The committee reviews each request based on the perspective of each member.

4. The committee either accepts/rejects the request or asks for more information.

5. All forms are maintained in a paper file.

6. Decisions are communicated to each sales

rep that must then inform
the customer and a proposal
is generated as appropriate.

Although this process is relatively straight forward, assume that 80 percent of the proposals require a special price approval and that 90 percent of the requests are approved. If the approval process consumes 16 hours per week and delays generation of an approved proposal by an average of 3-7 days.

Clearly, there are many issues associated with this process. The high percentage of requests indicates that either the pricing is wrong or the sales force is not doing a good job of selling value. Since 90 percent of the requests are approved, one must conclude that the field is requesting reasonable deviations. This suggests more latitude with pricing and an improved qualification of what constitutes the 10 percent that are rejected. The remaining 20 percent that truly need review to cull out the faulty 10 percent could be run through the same process with significantly less resources being involved. Most important of all, the customer will experience significantly less delay in obtaining pricing information.

After plotting the flow diagram, it is often useful to summarize the process as follows:

Process Step	Description	Process Time (Hr's)	Work Time (Hr's)	Value Added Time (Hr's)	Volume
1					
2					
3					
4					
5					
6					

Process time is essentially elapsed or cycle time. Work time is the hours associated with completing that step and value added time is processing time that adds value from a stakeholder perspective. A step is considered non-value added if it meets any of the following criteria:

■ If the stakeholder is a customer, a non-value added step is one for which the customer is not willing to pay. The step does not change the work output in a way that makes the output more valuable to the customer.

■ The step does not contribute positively to the requirements of one or more of the other stakeholders.

■ The process step does not contribute to the effectiveness, efficiency, or flexibility of the process.

In general, sub-process analysis should identify opportunities to eliminate steps or entire processes. The result should be shorter cycle time, improved output quality, and reduced sales and staff resource requirements. Given this level of documentation, it should be straightforward to claim savings from internal staff reduction or cost avoidance.

11

Continuous Improvement

In Chapter 1 it was stressed that there are two components to the benefits associated with justifying a CRM system. One benefit is the immediate improvement that can be predicted based on current planning. The other benefit is the data that the system provides and the impact it can have given that the organization pursues a continuous improvement program.

The responsibility for continuous improvement is typically assigned to a group of individuals representing the functions that touch the customer or otherwise impact the sales process. Since this group must work together to improve performance, it must have a set of tools that help it to function. Fortunately, the manufacturing function wrestled with the issue of group problem solving during the late 1970's. The result of this effort was the development of a powerful set of tools that help group problem solving to be both efficient and effective. This chapter is designed to provide an overview of these techniques; further definition can be derived by referencing most texts on Total Quality Management (TQM).

The Basic Techniques

Brainstorming: This is a free wheeling technique for generating ideas. The ideas are captured on a flip chart. No one is allowed to critique an idea but questions of clarification are welcomed. When ideas have been exhausted, the list is reviewed and the options prioritized using a voting technique. Brainstorming is most useful when the objective is to generate a list of ideas, problems, or potential solutions.

Data Collection: Sampling surveys, check sheets, and other data collection tools are used to gather data regarding a situation or event.

The data can then be plotted on graphs. The most common types of graphs are called histograms and scatter diagrams.

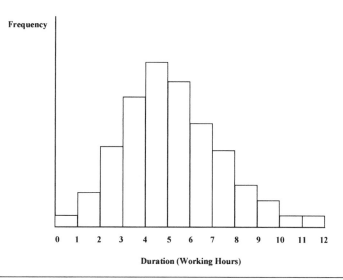

Figure 11.1 Example of a histogram

For example, the histogram in figure 11.1 could represent the distribution of cycle times for generating a proposal. Interestingly, most organizations would not be aware of the length of time required to generate a proposal; therefore, they lack a starting place to assess the problem. Once the distribution is known, brain storming can be used to identify reasons for the different cycle times. The team can then identify methods for eliminating sources of delay.

A scatter diagram is used to look for a relationship between two variables. For example, suppose that the sales team thought there is a relationship between the cycle time to generate proposals and closing the deal. The team could plot the data as provided in figure 11.2.

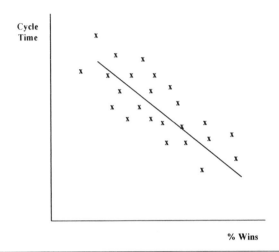

Figure 11.2 Example of a scatter diagram

The graph in figure 11.2 clearly shows a relationship between percent wins and cycle time. Thus, if the CRM system can reduce the cycle time to generate proposals, the result should be an increased close rate or more revenue per sales rep.

A third type of chart is referred to as a Pareto diagram. It is named after a statistician who discovered that 80 percent of a country's wealth was in the hands of 20 percent of the people. This idea of concentrated effect has carried over to industry, for example, 80 percent of a company's revenue is typically associated with 20 percent of the customers.

Pareto analysis is often used for prioritization. Suppose a sales team was investigating the source of errors associated with orders, they would probably discover many types of errors. Errors could include wrong purchase order number, missing purchase order number, transposition or part number, wrong quantity, etc. A logical question would be what problems represent the majority of the errors? A Pareto chart could be used to identify and communicate the errors that contribute to 80 percent of the mistakes. As the analysis in figure 11.3

suggests, correcting no part number, transposition of part no., and missing quantity would eliminate 80 percent of the errors found. An order entry system would no doubt provide this type of editing. The result would be reduced order processing time and effort.

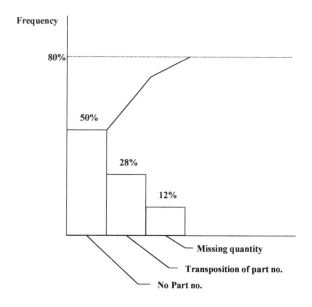

Figure 11.3 Example of a Pareto chart

Cause – Effect (Fishbone) Analysis

The concept of the cause and effect diagram is to integrate brainstorming within a context or discipline. The context is created by the fishbone structure as indicated in figure 11.4.

The analysis starts by identifying a specific problem, issue, or goal. For example, the issue could be lower than desired average margins. The next step would be to identify the major groupings (bones on the fish), in this case we will chose training, manpower, support, and tools.

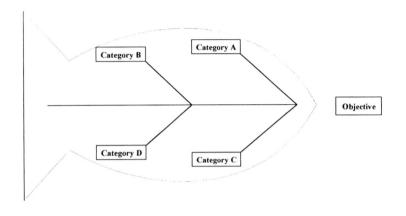

Figure 11.4 Format for a cause and effect (fishbone) analysis

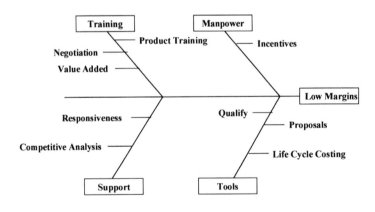

Figure 11.5 Cause – effect analysis of the issue of low margins

Brainstorming regarding the low margin issue could include the following:

Manpower
The incentive system emphasizes revenue not margins or profitability

Tools
Prospect qualifying does not include an emphasis on value based buying strategies
Proposal format lacks a strong case to support the price
The reps lack tools to demonstrate life cycle costing

Training
Sales reps need more product training to better position the products
There is no standard negotiation process
Sales reps are inconsistent in their ability to demonstrate value-added features to the prospect

Support
Technical support is not responsive to field sales questions
There is no centralized database with competitive information and no one is responsible for competitive analysis.

The sales team would then vote on those items, which they think, have the most impact on low margins. These prioritized items will then be investigated for further action.

Statistical Control
Most of the techniques outlined in this chapter are based on using group processes to identify issues and potential solutions. These methods are static in nature, in that they are applied at one point in time; but how does one know that the process is operating "correctly" after the action is taken? One of the techniques used in the discipline of Quality is known as Statistical Quality Control and it provides a mechanism that aids decision making relative to when to take action and when a process is ready for change. Before embarking on this discussion, it should be mentioned that there are hundreds of books written on this subject; therefore, this section is intended to provide a very cursory overview of

the subject. The reader is encouraged to review the bibliography for suggested further reading on this subject.

The statistical control concept can be described in terms of a run chart. A run chart is simply a graph that plots the results of measurement from a process over time. The following graph describes a run chart.

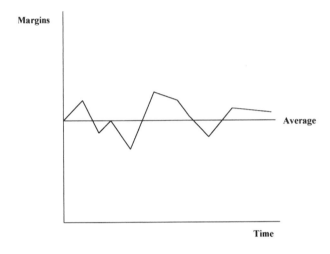

Figure 11.6 Example of a run chart

The run chart provides a graphical representation of the behavior of this process over time. Note that one could take this same type of information and convert it into a bar chart (histogram) format. An example of this is provided in figure 11.7.

The chart in figure 11.7 reflects an obvious trend that is not detected by the histogram; so examining data via a run chart provides significant insight relative to the behavior of the process. The run chart however does not reveal when action is required and the type of action required. This is where statistics come into play. Statistical analysis reveals that random variations within a process will cause the results to vary within a specific range of values relative to the average value. An upper

control limit (UCL) and a lower control limit (LCL) define this range.
The form that a statistical control chart takes is indicated in figure 11.8.

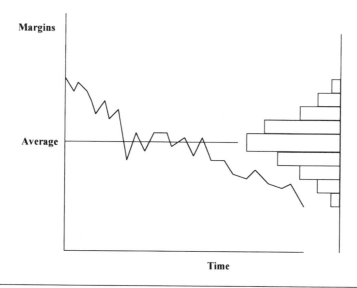

Figure 11.7 Insight gained by a run chart versus a histogram

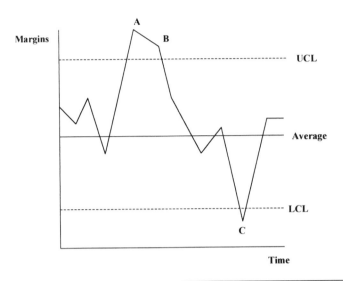

Figure 11.8 Example of a statistical control chart

The field of statistical quality control provides significant guidance regarding the determination of whether a process is reflecting random variation within the system or if there is cause of variation that lies outside the system. For the purposes of this discussion, it is sufficient to understand that when values fall outside the control limits (points A, B, and C), the likelihood is very high that the cause is assignable (i.e. other than random variation) and needs to be rectified. Thus, this process facilitates decision making relative to when to take corrective action.

A stable process, one with no indication of assignable cause of variation, is said to be in statistical control or *stable*. The behavior of such a process is subject to random variation and is therefore **predictable**. This is a key concept, because true improvement of a process can only occur if it is predictable i.e. results occur within certain capabilities.

Given these concepts, how does one improve a process (or demonstrate predictable improvement)? There are essentially three phases to this improvement process:

Phase I: Establish a measurement system and plot the data on a run chart using statistically derived upper and lower control limits.

Phase II: Investigate and eliminate assignable causes as identified by the control chart so that process stability is achieved.

Phase III: Improve the process by studying and eliminating sources of variation within the system; this will result in improvement in the average and reduction in the span of the control limits. Under these conditions, the process has been improved in a predictable manner.

Potential Applications of Statistical Control

Statistical control is a very powerful tool for improving the level of performance and predictability of processes. The technique could be applied to a process such as order entry. Identification of the frequency and types of errors would be very helpful to improving the cycle time and resource commitment associated with this process. Automation of the process could further enhance performance through the introduction of edits and logic that essentially eliminate common errors by sales reps.

Another interesting application of statistical control is in the area of total revenue. Consider the differences in performance of the two hypothetical companies portrayed in figure 11.9.

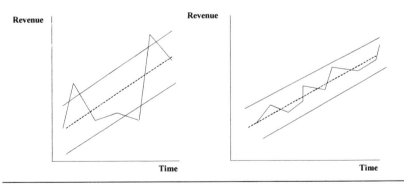

Figure 11.9 Comparison of revenue variability of two companies

Companies A and B are growing at the same rate. However, the revenue behavior of company B is within a much more narrow range and the process is in control; therefore, it is predictable. Company B will experience smoother operations and most likely require less inventory for the same level of sales as company A. The net impact of these differences should be higher profitability and return on investment.

Consider the impact of CRM systems, does automation of the sales process and sub-processes reduce the variability associated with revenue generation? This is a fairly new and unexplored aspect of CRM systems, the impact for organizations could be large.

Success Stories

In his book, *Sales, Marketing, and Continuous Improvement*, Daniel Stowell summarizes a research study involving over sixty companies that have effectively integrated continuous improvement into their sales and marketing function[4]. These companies spanned a wide range of industries and were of varying size; thus, the conclusions are generally applicable.

According to Stowell's research, six practices could be identified as being common to the most successful efforts:
- Manage for change
- Listen to customers
- Focus on process
- Use of teams
- Proactive and open organizational cultures
- Apply technology

The situation for many of these companies was similar to that revealed by Dartnell's surveys. Sales people spend about half of their time in non-selling related activities. Companies with improvement processes experienced 16 percent of sales time associated with fixing

---

[4] Stowell, Daniel M., *Sales, Marketing, and Continuous Improvement*, Jossey-Bass Publishers San Francisco, 1997.

things while those companies without improvement processes expended 28 percent of sales time dedicated to this same purpose.

Harte-Hanks Direct Marketing discovered that the average value of a customer was $275 each whereas the top 10 percent customers averaged $3450 each and that 11 percent of the top customers were defecting each year. The company immediately adopted a customer retention program for the top tier customers.

In a 1992 unpublished internal study by IBM, management found that sales organizations that embraced Baldrige criteria outperformed those that did not. The successful ones generally achieved 30% plus growth in sales, market share, and profitability over those that did not follow the Baldrige criteria. Thus, for example, an IBM sales organization that expanded market by 3 percent and did not apply Baldrige principles essentially failed to gain an additional 1 percent growth in market share. *The evidence was so dramatic that the corporation insisted that all sales organizations worldwide speed up their implementation of quality practices.*

IBM Wisconsin started an initiative in response to a recognized need to change the focus of the sales organization. A vision statement was created which positioned the company as not only selling computers to data centers, but also to *help customers gain competitive advantage* in the worldwide market.

In response to this vision, four steps were taken immediately:

1. The six branch offices were given one quota to encourage offices to work as a team.
2. The number of managers was *reduced* to facilitate a flatter organization and *empowerment*.
3. An educational program was started.
4. A new compensation system was developed which rewards revenue contribution, customer satisfaction improvement, leadership, and skills development.

The surveys indicated that customers wanted: 1) reps with better skills and 2) an easier company to do business with. One of the changes involved the pooling of the technical services organization so that the right resource would be available at the right place. Within six months, the technical consulting services organization *increased contract work revenue by more than 100%.*

In summary, the organization identified four lessons:

1. Senior management must support the market driven quality movement.
2. Employees closest to the customer know what changes need to be made.
3. Enormous investment in education.
4. Performance measures and compensation must be changed to reward individuals for improving customer satisfaction.

Eastman Chemical Corporation was one of the winners of the 1993 Malcolm Baldrige Quality Award. Their Total Quality Management Process started with a review and assessment of customer relationships and opportunities for improvements. The company is committed to making improvements in these areas and reporting back to their customers.

The sales organization contracts with the company's ten separate (and diverse) business units. The sales organization is charged with implementing all of those strategies. In support of the TQM process, the sales people often find themselves in the position of coordinating many of Eastman's employee team efforts focused on improving customer relationships. This is referred to as "linking in" the sales function into the quality effort. The overall program is called "MEPS", Make Eastman the Preferred Supplier. Two valuable tools for determining customer satisfaction are the complaint process and the customer satisfaction survey. In the past, Eastman observed that it would require the equivalent of three meetings to decide that an item should be added to the complaint file. This quickly changed under the new mind-set and Eastman now makes it easy or customers to register complaints. One indication that the quality system is working is that in the past two years, claims and returns have decreased by 40%.

Customer surveys are sent out on an 18-month cycle. Performance factors include order entry/processing, on-time delivery, product quality, pricing practice, new products, management contacts, and sharing of market information. It is the responsibility of the sales rep to go back to the customer and discuss the survey results and to disclose improvement efforts completed and underway.

Based on the examples provided in this chapter, continuous improvement offers a great deal of potential for the sales and marketing arena. However, this is the subject of entire books, therefore the intent is to provide the reader with an overview. See the bibliography for more references to this topic.

12

Total Costs

Many CRM initiatives fail due to inadequate planning or assessment of the commitment. As the reality of inadequate resource allocation becomes apparent, project teams tend to cut corners and that leads to failure. Since this book is meant to guide justification, this chapter is designed to help the reader understand and therefore better estimate the true costs of development, implementation, and maintenance for the proposed system.

It is very difficult to identify every cost for every type of company/industry hence this chapter needs to be viewed as a thought provoker and not as a checklist. The following list identifies the major elements of the typical phased installation. Obviously, each phase will have a corresponding cost. Each company has different attitudes regarding the inclusion of internal resources in project costs. Note that typically there will be an internal project manager and an external project manager representing one or more vendors; project management will be mentioned at each section as well as project team members.

The Needs Assessment
- Resources:
    - ❖ Project Manager(s)
    - ❖ Project Team (internal and external members)
    - ❖ Field Sales time
- Field "Workwiths"
- Focus group sessions with stakeholders
- Customer Interviews
- Meeting days
- Travel costs
- Presentation material
- Software/hardware for demonstration purposes

■ Notes: Travel costs can be exceptionally high during this phase. Field input is essential which means people are going out to the field or field people are coming in for group discussion.

Change Management
■ Resources
  ❖ Project Manager(s)
  ❖ Project Team (internal and external members)
  ❖ Field Sales time
  ❖ Human Resources Department
  ❖ Training Department
  ❖ Change consultants
■ Field surveys
■ Program planning
■ Interim training
■ Field communications
■ Focus group sessions
■ Methods for follow-up training
■ Metrics for user acceptance

System Design and Development
■ Resources:
  ❖ Project Manager(s)
  ❖ Project Team (internal and external members)
  ❖ Travel
  ❖ Field Sales time
■ User System
  ❖ Functional specifications
  ❖ Design specifications
  ❖ Development: iterative process
  ❖ Laptop computers and software
  ❖ Testing
  ❖ Documentation
■ Server System
  ❖ Functional specifications
  ❖ Design specifications
  ❖ Development

- ❖ Server, software, and modems
- ❖ Install communication lines
- ❖ Communications costs
- ❖ Testing
- ❖ Documentation
- ■ Data Base
  - ❖ Functional specifications
  - ❖ Design specifications
  - ❖ Development
  - ❖ Software
  - ❖ Testing
  - ❖ Documentation
- ■ Interface With Legacy Systems
  - ❖ Functional specifications
  - ❖ Design specifications
  - ❖ Development
  - ❖ Software
  - ❖ Hardware/software to link systems
  - ❖ Testing
  - ❖ Documentation
  - ❖ Notes: Critical aspects of this phase are that the end user interface design process is iterative, there can be many meetings and travel associated with this activity. Although the connection to the legacy systems is referred to as an interface, the reality is that these systems may require more than a simple utility program to extract or add data. Major funding can be involved in this area

Pilot Preparation
- ■ Resources:
  - ❖ Project Manager(s)
  - ❖ Project Team (internal and external members)
  - ❖ Travel
  - ❖ Field Sales time
- ■ Training Concept and Materials
  - ❖ Define training content and approach
  - ❖ Develop training scenario's (day in the life concept)

- ❖ Document approach and produce materials
- ❖ Dry runs
- ❖ Define training site requirements, review adequacy of pilot training location and test communication capabilities
- ❖ Finalize materials
- ❖ Notes: Companies typically underestimate their training budgets by a factor of four. Include cost factors such as sales person costs, instructor costs, facilities costs, and materials costs.

■ Data Preparation
- ❖ Convert data to load into modules
- ❖ Testing
- ❖ Notes: This step includes e-mail lists, customer data, reference information, etc. Any type of information that can be pre-loaded in the software should be loaded to minimize the administrative requirements of the system. At the pilot stage, this conversion may be a more manual process and the insight gained should guide the rollout methodology. Some input by the reps will inevitably be required but even in this respect; there should be a time frame to complete it.

■ Purchase hardware, accessories, and software
- ❖ Notes: From a budgeting standpoint this can be tricky, the purchase will likely include more users than the field pilot group. Other people will need to be on the system such as project people, help line, perhaps other staff groups depending on the nature of the applications. Spare equipment will also be needed to cover equipment that fails. If changes in process are involved, steps must be taken to accommodate modifications for pilot evaluation and planning for the rollout.

■ Prepare hardware
- ❖ Burn-in equipment to reduce potential of field failures or DOA's at training
- ❖ Load software and data
- ❖ Add accessories
- ❖ Test software and communications
- ❖ Repackage (return to original packaging and over-wrap to provide a sales rep unit)

- ❖ Ship to training sites
- ❖ Notes: This set of activities can be full of surprises, equipment and software fail high costs for preparation and shipping. There must be secure places to store the equipment during preparation, and at the training site.
- ■ Establish services
  - ❖ Define requirements (hours of coverage, escalation, repair turnaround time, etc.)
  - ❖ Select vendor(s) and/or recruit internal resources
  - ❖ Train helpline staff regarding configuration and unique applications
  - ❖ Add full time IS staff to run the system (may not be necessary)
  - ❖ Inventory all equipment and setup tracking data base
  - ❖ Notes: The pilot is a live operation. It needs to be complete so that the adequacy of the capabilities can be evaluated prior to rollout. The intent should be to avoid surprises at rollout. The implication of this is that operational costs will start to kick in even before the pilot starts, these costs will be disproportionately higher than the rollout because of economies of scale.
- ■ Define success criteria for the pilot

Pilot Operation

- ■ Resources:
  - ❖ Project Manager(s)
  - ❖ Project Team (internal and external members)
  - ❖ Travel
  - ❖ Field Sales time
  - ❖ Trainers and Services Support
  - ❖ Training facility costs
  - ❖ Operational costs including communication costs, support services etc.
  - ❖ IS Operations Staff
- ■ Conduct Training
- ■ Evaluate Training
- ■ Conduct field workwiths

- Formal evaluation of the pilot from an operational and performance standpoint
- Evaluate readiness for rollout
- Re-run, extend, expand pilot based on results
- Report readiness for rollout to senior management
- Notes: The pilot operation is critical to success. It is important not to allow schedules to get in the way of making sure that the methodology is right. The costs to fix problems, once they reach the field, are staggering not to mention the loss in credibility. Also note that when a pilot is set up, it typically stays in operation while preparations are made for the rollout, this means that the operating costs continue during this period.

Modification of Systems/Services

- Resources:
    - Project Manager(s)
    - Project Team (internal and external members)
    - Travel
    - Field Sales time
    - Trainers and Services Support
    - Training facility costs
    - Operational costs including communication costs, support services etc.
    - IS Operations Staff
    - Notes: Feedback from the pilot may reveal flaws in the system that need to be corrected before the pilot is launched. Sometimes these are modest in scope and can be handled during the pilot operation. Depending on the nature of the change, it may be wise to re-run or expand the pilot group to evaluate the merits of the change before rollout. These are judgment calls, but from a budgeting standpoint, failure to comprehend such an event will easily violate budget and time frame estimates.

Ramp Up For the Rollout

- Resources:
    - Project Manager(s)

- ❖ Project Team (internal and external members)
- ❖ Travel
- ❖ Field Sales time
- ❖ Trainers and Services Support
- ❖ Training facility costs
- ❖ Operational costs including communication costs, support services etc.
- ❖ IS Operations Staff
- ■ Develop logistics plan
  - ❖ Identify training sites and schedules (may involve site visits)
  - ❖ Identify trainers and develop train the trainer schedule
  - ❖ Develop equipment and software purchase schedule and establish secure area for holding prior to rollout.
  - ❖ Location, through-put and resources to meet rollout schedule
  - ❖ Shipment logistics to coordinate equipment with training sites.
  - ❖ Coordination of events with the field
  - ❖ Quality control to ensure smooth operation
- ■ Train the trainers
  - ❖ Interview and select trainers
  - ❖ Train the trainers
  - ❖ Schedule dry runs to determine readiness
- ■ Equipment and Software Preparation
  - ❖ Receive equipment and software enter in data base and secure for use
  - ❖ Prepare equipment for rollout training
  - ❖ Load software and data and re-pack
  - ❖ Ship to training sites according to schedule
- ■ Communicate with the organization as a whole, the schedule, expectations, etc.
- ■ Coordinate training schedule
  - ❖ Field users
  - ❖ Trainers
  - ❖ Internal staff users
  - ❖ Service providers

Execute Rollout

- Resources:
    - ❖ Project Manager(s)
    - ❖ Project Team (internal and external members)
    - ❖ Travel
    - ❖ Field Sales time
    - ❖ Trainers and Services Support
    - ❖ Training facility costs
    - ❖ Operational costs including communication costs, support services etc.
    - ❖ IS Operations Staff
- Notify senior management of readiness
- Notes: It is wise to maintain a modest backup group at headquarters that can scrabble to solve or correct any problems experienced in the field including sudden illness of trainers.

Post Rollout Review

- Resources:
    - ❖ Project Manager(s)
    - ❖ Project Team (internal and external members)
    - ❖ Travel
    - ❖ Field Sales time
    - ❖ Trainers and Services Support
    - ❖ Training facility costs
    - ❖ Operational costs including communication costs, support services etc.
    - ❖ IS Operations Staff
- Establish a punch list of outstanding issues and setup plans for corrective action
- Evaluate performance of the rollout
- Monitor usage of the system
- Conduct spot workwiths to evaluate system or organizational issues that need attention
- Report results to senior management
- Celebrate!!!
- Setup plans to re-absorb internal project resources

■ Notes: Again, from a budgeting standpoint, there must be a clear agreement when project mode is over and operational mode is in place. Project resources may require time to re-absorb so the project budget needs to reflect a continuation of resources to take care of loose ends and the re-absorption process.

On-going Maintenance

■ Resources:
- ❖ Project champion (may be part time)
- ❖ Operational resources
- ❖ Support services
- ❖ Training for new users
- ❖ Follow-up training as required
- ❖ Administrator(s) to maintain the system
- ❖ Operational budget
- ❖ Project budget to expand and enhance the system based on the original plan
- ❖ Capital budget to comprehend new users
- ❖ Communication budget to relate issues regarding success stories etc.

13

Building The Business Case

A CRM system represents a major investment and commitment for any organization. In addition to investment in the system, there is the issue of change management. There are always inherent risks associated with any major system installation and sales automation tends to impact a significant population of the organization; there is also a great deal at risk in terms of negatively effecting the sales function.

Since senior management will view sales force automation as both a source of opportunity and risk, a successful proposal must address these issues. The proposal must convince management that the benefits and risks associated with the proposal are more favorable than alternatives such as operating in the current mode of operation. The proposal must address key financial metrics while linking the benefits of the system to other management strategies as appropriate.

This chapter will provide an overview of where to look for linkage type of information and some general guidelines associated with sources of benefits related with sales systems.

Defining Current Assumptions

The primary concerns of senior management consist of issues such as:

- Revenue growth
- Market share
- Profitability
- Competitive advantage
- Organizational strategies
- Acquisitions/divestitures
- Valuation on the stock market

To start building the business case, review annual reports, the marketing plan, the strategic plan, product development plans, and budgets. What do these documents say about......

- Growth rates
- Profitability
- Acquisitions/divestitures
- Head count
- Key investment areas
- Key initiatives
- Strategies
- Assumptions?

Note that the definition of a **strategy** is a set of hypotheses about **cause and effect**. Thus, it is critical to identify, in as concrete terms as possible, what are the cause/effect relationships? This will help to build the business case.

Most corporate financial metrics can be segmented into the following categories:

- Margins
- Revenue levels and growth rates
- Profitability
- Return on assets

Market share is not included in the above metrics because revenue growth relative to industry growth is the basis for market share. Therefore, market share does not need to be a separate component.

The Linkage Starts

The next level of detail is to link the financial goals to customer goals. Customer goals typically include the following:

Customer Satisfaction: Does the company have a formal customer satisfaction program? Are the results linked to on-going revenue, margins, etc.?

New Customers: What portion of future revenue is dependent on the acquisition of new customers?

Share of Customer: Share of customer is defined as the share of the total available business that your company could do with a customer. Given anticipated revenue from new customers, the remainder must be derived from existing customers. Does this imply an increase in the share of each customer's business?

Customer Retention: Share of customer is highly correlated to customer retention. If there is turnover in the customer base, then share of customer must increase disproportionately, to compensate for these loses.

Profitability: This relates to the profitability of doing business with each customer. The profitability numbers reflect whether you are doing business with the right customers. Trends in this area indicate whether value added programs and strategies are working.

The linkage between these factors is graphically represented as follows:

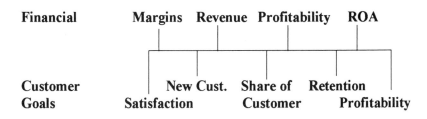

Figure 13.1 Linkage between corporate financial goals and customer based goals

If your company does not have these types of metrics, it suggests that it is not following a customer centric strategy. This is not catastrophic from a justification perspective; it merely eliminates one set of potential linkage with the financial goals.

The next level of linkage is with operational strategies. This may involve many functional groups, but for simplicity, one can think in terms of development, sales, marketing, and channel development. This interface is represented in figure 13.2.

Figure 13.2 Expanding the linkage of corporate goals to operational strategies

What are the specific strategies of these functional areas and how do they relate to customer goals and financial goals? The following discussion outlines some of the basic questions regarding these operational strategies:

Product Development: What is the projected rate of new product/service introductions? Who are the target users and what experience does the sales organization have with these users/industries? What is the product life cycle of these new products and how does the rate of market penetration effect revenue and margins? What impact does innovation have on company growth and profitability over the next three to five years?

Sales: Is the sales organization anticipating changes in structure, head count, training, emphasis, incentives, deployment, etc. that are targeted at leveraging growth/profitability? Do the budgets reflect these changes? How are the changes linked to performance? Do the sales strategies reflect the direction and implementation of innovation, marketing, and channel development?

Marketing: How are the marketing programs linked to performance? What portion of revenue can be attributable to promotions or programs? How does marketing evaluate the effectiveness of these programs? What assumptions are being made about sales force resource time and knowledge/skill levels? What are the metrics and investment associated with lead management? How much revenue is linked to new business secured through the lead generation system?

Customer Service: What is the role of customer service today versus in the future, for example is there an opportunity for cross-selling? Are the products being developed going to require a different level or type of support? Does the customer base desire more or less "hands on" interface? Can web type applications better support portions of the customer base?

Channel Development: What are the recruitment plans for new channel members and what implication does this have for sales rep response time? What is the impact on cost and margins?

Areas of Leverage

By expanding the structure provided in figure 13.2 it is possible to link the strategies directly to the sales process. This linkage is captured in figure 13.3.

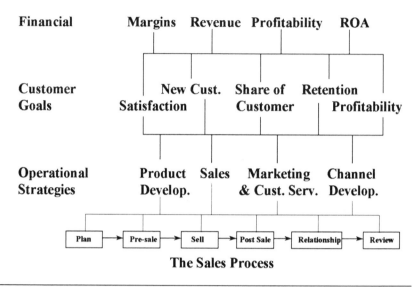

Figure 13.3 Expanding the linkage of corporate goals to the sales process

Areas of Leverage

Once the strategies have been articulated, it is possible to identify what the sales organization must do well for the organization to be successful. If these areas can be articulated, then it should be possible to identify areas within the sales process that support these capabilities and examine ways to strengthen them. This type of linkage is conceptually identified in figure 13.3. The following examples provide additional detail as to the linkage process.

Example of the Linkage: Revenue

In this example, a CRM system is used to improve the process of qualifying, distributing, and tracking of all leads generated by marketing.

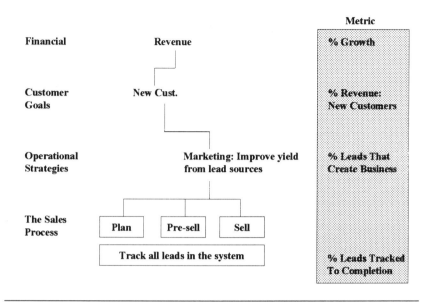

Figure 13.4 Example of linking corporate revenue goals to the sales process

Example of the Linkage: Margins

In this example, a CRM system is used to improve targeting and time allocation for accounts that recognize value added or are otherwise less price sensitive.

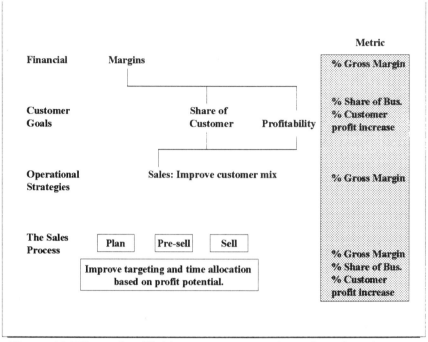

Figure 13.5 Example of linking corporate margin goals to the sales process

Example of the Linkage: Profitability

In this example, a CRM system is used to equip the Customer Service function to proactively cover selected accounts that can be better served by an inside sales effort. This allows the outside sales people to improve coverage of higher potential customers and prospects.

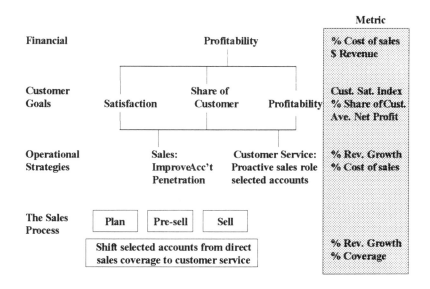

Figure No. 13.6 Example of linking corporate profitability goals to the sales process

Example of the Linkage: Return on Assets

There are many factors that influence return on assets. For example, increasing revenue growth and productivity can increase return on assets. However, one of the tangible ways in which a sales organization can impact return on assets is through the forecasting process. It is difficult to generalize about forecasting because companies have a wide variety of approaches. However, for many companies the process is time consuming and concludes with a result that no one is happy about. Part of the problem is that the forecasting approach typically requires the sales person to project revenue or units for their territory over a specific period of time. This tends to produce an arithmetic exercise that no one believes. An alternative is to recognize that there are two components of revenue (1) on-going or production volume and (2) new business. The basic question for the sales rep is:

■ Are there any anticipated changes in the level of production volume?

■ What new business is likely to close during the forecast planning horizon?

Asking these types of questions tapes into the knowledge area where the sales rep has unique insight. However, even with these basic questions the sales reps may tend to be overly optimistic or pessimistic. Therefore tools should be used at the headquarter level to net out this type of variation. Thus, the sales people should be the source of the input, but not necessarily the formulators of the forecast. Another tool for project probable new business is the population of proposals in the field. Some organizations have found that the population of proposals is a reasonable predictor of new business and to make some reasonable projections at the item level. The net of these techniques is to improve accuracy without adding a burden on the sales force.

The example in figure 13.7 is based on the assumption that having a CRM system will provide an inventory of all outstanding proposals and that this inventory will provide the basis to improve projections around new business.

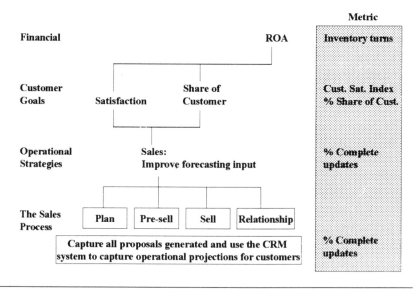

Figure 13.7 Example of linking corporate ROA goals to the sales process

Other Areas of Leverage

In general, the following areas are correlated with leveraging certain types of financial benefits.

Revenue

- Improvements in lead management will drive revenue by closing more new customers.
- Applications that help sales reps to increase share of customer's business will leverage revenue.
- Account targeting and coverage applications help to allocate overall time based on value or potential.
- Increased time for face to face calls should increase revenue.
- Opportunity management helps to focus sales reps on higher probability sales; thereby increasing revenue per sales rep.
- Reduction in sales rep turnover can reduce lost sales due to open territories while also reducing operational costs.
- Reduction in learning curve requirements for new reps or to learn to sell new products will result in increased overall productivity.

Margins

- Improvements in the mix of product and services can increase average margin.
- Changes in customer mix can improve margins if new customers buy on the basis of value and/or are capable of passing through price increases to their customer base.
- Effectively selling new products can raise margins if the new products have a superior margin position.
- Effectively selling a value added strategy will typically increase margins.
- Reduction in cycle time for key processes such as pricing, proposal generation, literature fulfillment, and sample management, can produce situations where the customer is less price sensitive.
- Incentives that emphasize margins versus revenue can reinforce margin increase strategies.

Profitability

For the purposes of this discussion, profitability will be considered as the equivalent of cost reduction or cost avoidance.

- Increased sales productivity can reduce the need to expand the sales force; thus, it is a cost avoidance.
- Eliminating paperwork and process steps while increasing accountability can reduce fulfillment and sample costs.
- The distribution of mail and reports electronically, can eliminate paper and mailing costs.
- Order entry related applications can reduce staff requirements and errors that increase costs in manufacturing.
- Reduction in on-site training can dramatically reduce training and travel costs.
- Increased customer retention can have significant leverage on organizational productivity.
- Elimination or streamlining of other sales related workflow can reduce costs by eliminating paper, forms, and head count (could be cost avoidance).

Return on Assets

- Return on assets can be leveraged either through increasing revenue disproportionately to asset increases or by reducing required assets. Since increasing revenue has already been discussed, the following comments will focus on areas that can be leveraged to reduce assets.
- Improved forecasting accuracy will result in lower raw material and finished goods inventory.
- Elimination of field sales offices can reduce assets.
- Improved management of consignment inventories will reduce the asset base.

Estimating Improvement Levels

Unlike manufacturing where detailed cost and performance metrics are maintained, the sales environment offers few benchmark figures to use for estimating. Where workflow is involved, it should be possible to accurately predict the reduction in man-hours associated with the changes. Reductions in cycle time, better targeting, etc., are more difficult to estimate in terms of incremental business. If raw data is available, it may be possible to use scatter diagrams to establish a relationship between the target improvement variable and revenue or margins. Lacking this type of data, one is left to informed estimates coming from sales and marketing. In general, small increases or decreases (percentage basis) when applied to large numbers will generate large numbers. For example, a tenth of a percent improvement in margin applied to a revenue base of $100 million is a $100,000 profit contribution.

One of the most difficult areas to estimate is the degree to which a reduction in non-selling time will be converted into productive sales time. Chapter 8 discussed this issue at some length.

14

Managing Risk

If one is acquainted with the sales force automation industry at all, it is hard to miss the surveys that suggest very high organizational failure rates. Even without these statistics to reinforce the point, sales force automation is a complex initiative that involves a sophisticated blend of technology, organizational change, and strategy. The stakes involve egos, investment, and performance that can literally make or break careers.

Given these sobering facts, why do companies still approach sales force automation as though it is a decision analogous to choosing the next car model for the sales fleet? Some possible explanations for such behavior include:

■ Management does not understand the breadth and depth of the investment or potential pay-out

■ Management does not perceive the degree of risk involved with the initiative

■ Management has a bias for action and does not believe that studying needs is productive

■ Management views sales force automation as a necessary but wish to minimize the expenditure.

These orientations are virtually guaranteed to place a sales force automation initiative on the casualty list. Cost minimization and not forming a solid definition of where the organization wants to be result in short cuts and unreasonable expectations that undermine system acceptance.

The secret to successful implementation is knowing where you are going, how you are going to get there, and how you will determine that you have arrived. This prescription suggests planning and prudent consensus building. The remainder of this chapter identifies some of the basic sources of risk and suggests project management strategies for managing risk.

The Pot Holes

The road to sales force automation has been traveled for over ten years and although the technology has been increasingly sophisticated, the recipe for success has remained unchanged and the things that go wrong are also unchanged. From the earliest days of the industry, vendors and consultants have pointed to the same prescription (10 do's of CRM):

- Gain top management support
- Seek early wins with reps
- Create a multi-disciplined team
- Introduce applications that work the way the rep works
- Address applications that the sales organization feels are a priority
- Involve field sales people in the design
- Pilot test all applications with clear success criteria
- Use quality training and invest in adequate training time
- Provide superior support-minimize problems
- Have a clear champion for the system

This type of admonishment is instructive but it is the view from 100,000 feet, from this elevation it is hard to see the potholes. More specific information is available through the Sales Automation Association, trade literature, newsletters, web sites, and trade shows (see appendix for specific references). Consultants are another source of this type of information but one must be cautious that the individual or group has significantly more experience than you do.

The objective of this chapter is to provide you with a general idea of the potholes that potentially swallow you up versus those which result in a bumpy ride. Given this information, it should be possible to assemble a plan of action similar to the recommendations in the last chapter (A Road Map).

Organizational Support

Sales force automation, by definition, implies organizational change. The change required has more far-reaching consequences than most people initially recognize. Change implies resistance (even if the change is perceived as positive) because it is disruptive. Therefore, the first task is to identify stakeholders within the organization who will be impacted by changes in the sales process and/or the technology. This will typically generate a list that includes functions such as:

Sales reps	Information Technology
Sales Management	Marketing
	Training
Customer Service	Finance
Engineering/Development	Channel Management

For each of these groups, one has to ask what are their needs and motivations versus fears and concerns? A comparable type of review must be done for each function. This information provides insight relative to their sense of "wins" while being sensitive regarding their perception of potential loss. It will require a team effort to be successful with sales force automation therefore skipping this step is fraught with risk.

Automating Broken Processes

Broken processes pertain to current processes that have not been defined reviewed, or studied. The topic of automating a sales force without defining the sales process has been identified several times. There are other classics, such as, automating a faulty forecasting process only to find out that the organization still gets lousy estimates, it just gets them faster!

Automating current practices may have some efficiency benefits but logic would suggest that improving the process in ways that leverage the benefit of the technology is preferable.

Vendor Selection

Selection of a vendor is critically important. This decision involves an evaluation of technology, financial strength, and vendor management. Since this is a very complex decision, one could easily write a book on this topic alone, but the following comments address some of the major issues:

1. Technology
- If possible, choose technology platforms that are industry standards and supported by your I.T. organization. Failure to do this will increase the risk of increased cost and difficulty supporting the system.
- Define requirements before looking at or evaluating vendors. Many companies have failed to do this only to realize that the system isn't scalable or is incapable of supporting a key function.
- Test the system via benchmarking or speaking to current customers to establish true capabilities.

2. Financial Strength
There have been a number of vendors that have been subsidiaries of major corporations, which have still left the marketplace due to performance issues. Thus, regardless of the source of financing, what is important to understand is the expectations of the owners, be they corporate parents or venture capitalists? In addition, if private ownership is involved, what are the criteria for cashing out the investment? Acquisition is the type of an event that can pre-occupy management and influence future behavior.

3. Management Strength
Does the organization appear to be dependent on one or two people? What type of bench strength do they have? Are key people likely to leave after an IPO etc.?

Cost Overruns

There are two basic sources of risk relative to cost, one is not including a vital element in the budget and the other is an over-run on a project element. Both of these situations are typically experienced at some level on every project. Chapter 12 attempts to provide help in terms of identifying cost line items but over-runs are difficult to anticipate. Including a contingency factor with the budget estimate is a wise thing to do but when all else fails, senior management must provide assistance and guidance in terms of prioritizing and providing additional funding. As indicated in Chapter 6, Senior Management support is critical, not only for financial reasons but also from an organizational commitment standpoint.

Reduced Benefits

Reduced benefits can arise from economic conditions, competitive activity, optimistic estimates, and non-use of the system. The first two items are beyond control, but the last two are potentially controllable from a risk standpoint. A disciplined approach and prioritizing end user preferred applications can significantly reduce risk.

As was discussed in Chapter 13, some estimates may be in the best guess category but for processes that represent workflows, analysis of benefits should be quite accurate. Market related estimates such as margin improvement, where possible, should be subjected to scatter diagram type of analysis. The scatter diagram will indicate whether there is reason to believe that there is a relationship between the variable in question and margins achieved. Even if this analysis shows a strong relationship with margins, it is wise to be conservative with such estimates. Market success, may be countered by competitive reaction, that in the short run, dilutes impact.

Return on Investment

It would be quite easy to state that return on investment is a composite of the risks associated with costs and benefits but there is also the issue of under investing and over investing. Theoretically, the result of under or over investing is a return of zero; however, a more realistic view of sales force automation is captured in figure 14.1.

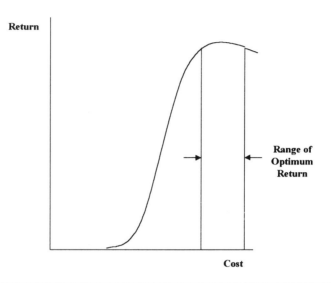

Figure 14.1 The range of optimum return

For any given organization, there is a range of investment that maximizes return. To find this optimum point, applications and their impact need to be prioritized so that the point of diminishing return is apparent. This handles the financial implementation; however, there is a risk factor associated with what applications are provided to the field sales force and in what order they are introduced. It should be self explanatory that return on investment is tightly coupled with proper usage of the system by sales reps. Given this dependency, it makes sense to roll out applications that the sales reps desire regardless of the return in the short run. This strategy can dilute return on investment for the project but reduce the probability of a lower return based on non-use of the system.

A Risk Management Methodology

A sales automation initiative can be segmented into three distinct phases:
- Needs analysis
- Pilot
- Phased Rollout

The needs analysis phase consists of all of the steps covered in this book. It defines the rationale for implementing a CRM system and provides an implementation plan and cost justification document. These three documents form the basis for gaining approval for the initiative.

During the pilot phase, the system design and development work is completed and the system is released to a limited number of users for pilot evaluation. It is assumed the pilot training and support exactly match the approach proposed for the rollout. The significance of this assumption is that if a different approach is used for the pilot, then the rollout takes on a different risk profile due to a lack of field trial and experience.

The rollout is referred to as a *phased* rollout because in most circumstances, functionality is given to the field sales force in a wave or phase fashion.

The relationship between the phases and risk management can be described graphically:

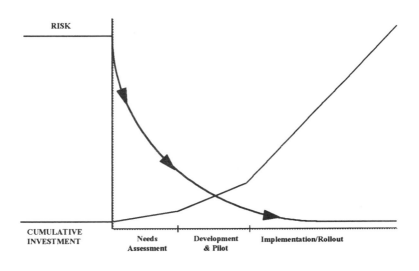

Figure 14.2 Risk versus phased investment

The vertical axis on this graph represents risk and cumulative investment and the horizontal axis represents time segmented into the three phases of the project. Note that during the needs analysis phase, the risk level drops significantly while the investment curve increased very gradually relative to the total investment. The rationale for this relationship is that a properly conducted assessment has a relatively small cost while its impact is to drive down risk by answering the questions of who, what, why, and how. The pilot phase involves significant fixed costs associated with the design and development of the system and training; therefore, the cumulative cost curve increases at a faster rate but is still small relative to the total. This phase answers the question regarding user acceptance and the adequacy of the training/support systems. The user acceptance question represents a significant risk potential; therefore, the risk curve is again reduced substantially. During the rollout phase, the cumulative investment increases substantially because of the high per user costs (laptop, software, support, etc.). At this stage, the risk curve flattens out; the rationale for this is that the remaining risk should essentially be associated with the logistics of the rollout. Thus, if properly executed, the risks associated with the greatest investment should be the most controllable i.e. logistics.

Thus, there is a disciplined methodology that provides a milestone approach to risk. If properly followed, the methodology should significantly reduce risk while leveraging the benefits of the system.

15

Project Evaluation and Approval

As was described in Chapter 4, getting your project included in the capital plan is an essential but not final step in the process. Before funding is released for a specific project, the project must be approved. At the level of investment for most CRM projects, this approval is at the Board of Directors level. To gain this level of approval, one must complete a formal request or project approval document. Most companies have very specific policies and forms associated with this process. Due to the special nature of this process, it is wise to consult with someone who has experience with successful submissions. Often this will be someone in finance, manufacturing, or information technology.

Also keep in mind that for many companies, the process is oriented toward manufacturing or building type of expenditures. The forms tend to emphasize cost savings rather than revenue generating initiatives; you will need to help the person you are working with understand the context of your estimates.

Since these funding decisions may not be considered more frequently than quarterly, it is imperative that you understand the timing of the events and get your submission completed early enough to meet these deadlines. It is also critical to keep senior management informed regarding the timing because approval may involve some "greasing of the skids." When the project is approved, you will be notified and a formal project number and project accounting system will be put in place to track the charges.

The following discussion is to provide an overview of how corporations examine major capital expenditures. It is not meant to be comprehensive, but rather to provide sufficient insight so that you can be more helpful to the individual who is preparing the submission.

The Time Value of Money

The whole premise of the analysis is built around the concept of the time value of money; in other words, a dollar received today is worth more than a dollar received a year from now (due to the ability to invest the dollar received today). Given this orientation, the analysis will focus on when cash flows out of the organization (expenditures) and when benefits are derived (savings or incremental revenue/margin). This analysis can be graphically represented as follows:

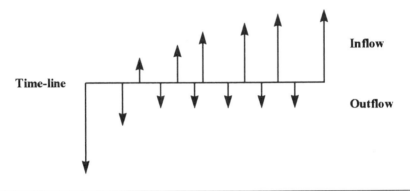

Figure 15.1 Graphical description of cash flow

Each arrow in figure 15.1 represents a movement of cash into or out of the organization. The height of the arrow is meant to represent the size of the cash flow. The basic questions are:

■ Will the size and timing of the inflows more than compensate for the size and timing of the outflows?

■ Are there alternative uses of this money that have a more attractive return?

Evaluation Techniques

Given that every project will have a different life cycle and flow of cost and benefits, how can one compare or otherwise evaluate these complex expenditures? Essentially, there are two methods of evaluation, they are referred to as net present worth and rate of return. Net present worth is based on an the use of a desired interest rate (each corporation has a unique rate based on the cost of raising capital) and discounts each cash flow (in and out) to its equivalent value if that transaction were to occur today. If the present worth exceeds zero, then the project meets the minimum acceptable criteria but that does not guarantee approval. If the company has limited funds and many projects, the choice would go to the projects with the highest net present worth (assuming a strictly analytical basis).

The other technique is referred to as a rate of return analysis. The rate of return is that level of interest that would cause the net present worth to be zero. This rate is then compared to a "hurdle rate" which is the minimum acceptable rate of return for the corporation.

Both techniques can be viewed as a go/no-go threshold; however, net present worth provides a stronger differentiation between projects because it reflects more of the financial impact of the investment. It should be mentioned that most corporations perform the analysis on an after tax basis. This means that the effect of depreciation will be factored into the cash flow. Details relative to depreciation and the salvage value of software and hardware at the end of the planning horizon and tax rates are best obtained from the financial department.

An Example
Suppose that a company is evaluating two projects that both require an initial investment of $2 million with subsequent costs of operation equal to $.75 million over a five year period. Benefits associated with the two projects however differ as indicated below ($ millions):

Year	1	2	3	4	5	Total
Project 1	.4	.8	1.2	2.4	4.8	9.6
Project 1	1.9	1.9	1.9	1.9	2.0	9.6

Using the graphical format used earlier, the flow for the projects appears as indicated in figure 15.2.

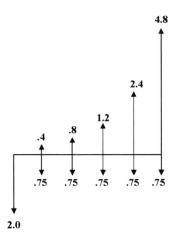

Figure 15.2 Cash flow for Project No. 1

Year	0	1	2	3	4	5	Total
Net Flow	-2.0	-.35	.05	.45	1.65	4.05	3.85

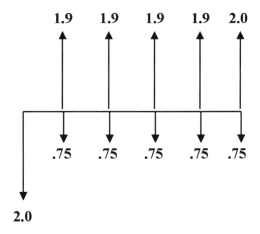

Figure 15.3 Cash flow for Project No. 2

Year	0	1	2	3	4	5	Total
Net Flow	-2.0	1.15	1.15	1.15	1.15	1.25	3.85

Suppose that the company is question uses a *hurdle* (minimum acceptable return) rate of 15 percent. This translates into a standard set of discount factors that convert the annual net cash flow to an equivalent amount of money in today's dollars.

Applying these factors, generates the following results:

Project No. 1

Year	0	1	2	3	4	5	Totals
Net Flow	-2.0	-.35	.05	.45	1.65	4.05	3.85
Discount Factor	1	.870	.756	.658	.572	.497	
Net Amount	-2.0	-.30	.04	.3	.94	2.01	.99

Project No. 2

Year	0	1	2	3	4	5	Totals
Net Flow	-2.0	1.15	1.15	1.15	1.15	1.25	3.85
Discount Factor	1	.870	.756	.658	.572	.497	
Net Amount	-2.0	1.00	.87	.76	.66	.62	1.90

As indicated by this analysis, Project 2 has a net present worth nearly double that of Project 1, despite the fact that the two projects have exactly the same investment and non-discounted value. The difference of course is the timing of the benefits.

The other evaluation technique is referred to as a rate of return. As indicated previously, the rate of return is that discount rate that causes the net present worth for the project to be zero. Using the same figures derived above, Project 1 has a rate of return of approximately 25 percent whereas Project 2 has a rate of return of over 50 percent. Using either criterion would favor Project 2.

16

An Example

Colossal Industries manufactures electro-mechanical devices that it sells to original equipment manufacturers (OEM's) and end user organizations that purchase the OEM's product. The company sells its products through a direct sales force that includes 100 sales people and ten managers. Total sales for the company is $200 million. Margins are currently at 28 percent, below the targeted level of 30 percent. The company has experienced increased competition as manufacturers emulate the innovations of Colossal. Never the less, the company is projecting a growth rate of 20 percent over the next five years. Colossal has 25 customer service people who enter orders and answer questions regarding the status of orders, ship dates, and/or complaints. For planning purposes, the company is assuming zero inflation with 4 percent productivity increases within sales and customer service.

	Year 1	Year 2	Year 3	Year 4	Year 5
Revenue	200	240	288	346	415
Margins	28%	28%	28%	28%	28%
Revenue per sales rep	2.0	2.1	2.2	2.2	2.3
No. of Sales reps*	100	115	133	154	177
Revenue per CS Rep	8.0	8.3	8.7	9.0	9.4
No. of CS reps*	25	29	33	38	44
Sales Managers 10:1 ratio	10	11	13	15	17
CS Managers 10:1 ratio	2	3	3	4	4

* Net of annual 4 percent productivity increase.

To make the math simple, assume that the Colossal sales reps earn a flat rate (salary and benefits) of $150,000 per year and that the customer service people earn $40,000 per year. This information supports the following base line projections ($ in millions). Assuming that it costs $40,000 per sales rep to hire and train a new rep, the net profit projection for Colossal based on the inflation and productivity figures provided would be as follows:

	Year 1	Year 2	Year 3	Year 4	Year 5
Revenue	200	240	288	346	415
Gross Margin	56.0	67.2	80.6	96.9	116.2
Less Salary & Benefits for Sales Reps	15.0	17.3	20.0	23.1	26.6
Less Training for Sales Reps		.6	.7	.8	.9
Less Salary & Benefits for CS Reps	1.0	1.2	1.3	1.5	1.8
Less Sales & CS Management	1.8	2.1	2.4	2.9	3.1
Net profit contribution	38.2	46.0	56.2	68.6	83.8

Colossal has just completed a needs assessment study. The study provided the following details:

1. Outside sales reps are completely dependent on the customer service reps for information regarding new orders and the status of orders. Checking order status represents 5 percent of time during normal working hours for the sales rep. The burden on the customer service reps is estimated at 15 percent due to the fact that there are more outside reps and some of the inquiries require research.

It was generally agreed that a daily order status report would eliminate the vast majority of this communication requirement. The results of this change have been estimated to be a 3 percent increase in sales rep productivity and a 12 percent increase in customer service productivity.

2. Due to paper based systems and "milk run" coverage patterns, sales reps are not penetrating the market as quickly as required when new products are introduced. This reduces the period when a more premium margin can be achieved and held through the product life cycle. The company feels that improved targeting could improve average margins by .2 percent.

3. Since much of the projected growth is expected to be derived through new customers, lead management is a key contributor to success. Currently, no statistics are maintained relative to success or close rates on leads but it is estimated that 5 percent of leads result in business and that the sales force is spending 15 percent of its time processing leads. Currently, leads are four weeks old before they reach the field. Automating the process should reduce this cycle time to three days. This is expected to leverage sales rep productivity by 3 percent.

4. The needs assessment also noted that it requires three weeks, on average, to create a prototype or sample for a customer. The sales organization feels that if the cycle time was reduced to one week it would increase opportunity closes by 20 percent and increase average margins by a net of .1 percent (increased responsiveness would equate to less price sensitivity). The net effect for the sales force would be a 5 percent increase in productivity and a .1 percent increase in margins.

5. Summary

	Sales Rep Productivity	CS Rep Productivity	Margins
Order Status	3	12	
Targeting			.2
Lead Management	3		
Prototype Development	5		.1
Totals	11%	12%	.3%

Assuming that it requires one year to design, pilot, and rollout the system, typically only a small percentage of the benefits are achieved in year one of the project. To be conservative, estimate that 75 percent of the benefits will be derived during year 2; this is equivalent to an 8 percent increase in sales rep productivity, a 9 percent increase in customer service productivity and a .2 percent increase in margins. The remaining benefits are derived in year No. 3.

Productivity improvements are typically best represented as a jump in productivity followed by the historical rate of improvement. The diagram below illustrates this phenomenon:

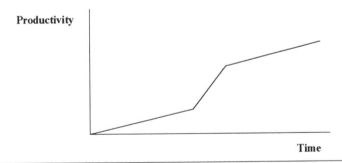

Figure 16.1 Productivity improvement scenario

Given these assumptions the reference numbers would appear as follows:

	Year 1	Year 2	Year 3	Year 4	Year 5
Revenue	200	240	288	346	415
Margins*	28%	28.2%	28.3%	28.3%	28.3%
Revenue per sales rep	2.0	2.2	2.4	2.5	2.6
No. of Sales reps**	100	109	120	138	160
Revenue per CS Rep	8.0	9.0	9.7	10.0	10.5
No. of CS reps**	25	26	29	34	39
Sales Management 10:1 ratio	10	11	12	14	16
CS Management 10:1 ratio	2	2	3	3	4

*Reflects incremental margin increase of .2% in year 2 and .1% in year 3 and beyond.
** Includes the incremental productivity increase plus the annual increase of 4 %.

	Year 1	Year 2	Year 3	Year 4	Year 5
Revenue	200	240	288	346	415
Gross Margin	56.0	67.7	81.5	97.9	117.4
Less Salary & Benefits for Sales Reps	15.0	16.3	18.0	20.7	24.0
Less Training for Sales Reps		.4	.4	.7	.9
Less Salary & Benefits for CS Reps	1.0	1.0	1.2	1.4	1.6
Less Sales & CS Management	1.8	2.0	2.3	2.6	3.0
Net profit contribution	38.2	48.0	59.6	72.5	87.9

Investment

Assume that the investment ($ millions) associated with the system including support requirements is as follows:

	Year 1	Year 2	Year 3	Year 4	Year 5
System investment, support & maintenance	1.5	.7	.8	.9	1.0

Note that the maintenance and support base for the system is assumed to be $.5 million per year. The post installation numbers reflect the incremental investment and maintenance associated with adding new users to the system.

It is very difficult to benchmark investment figures because the investment and maintenance costs are highly sensitive to assumptions regarding the linkage of the system to legacy systems.

Return Calculations

	Year 1	Year 2	Year 3	Year 4	Year 5	Total
Net profit contribution: with automation	38.2	48.0	59.6	72.5	87.0	306.2
Less net profit contribution: without automation	38.2	46.0	56.2	68.6	83.8	292.8
Incremental improvement		2.0	3.4	3.9	4.1	13.4
Incremental costs	(1.5)	(.7)	(.8)	(.9)	(1.0)	(4.9)
Net benefit	(1.5)	1.3	2.6	3.0	3.1	8.5

Assume that the before tax hurdle rate for the corporation is 15 percent, how would we calculate the present worth for this project?

The discount factors can be referenced in any book on ROI analysis, but these factors can be derived using the formula $1/(1 + i)^n$. Where i = the hurdle rate (decimal equivalent) and n = the number of years hence when the benefit will be received or the cost incurred. The more distant the value, the higher the discount.

Given this discounting mechanism, a conservative approach to costs and benefits is to assume that all costs begin at the beginning of the year in which they are incurred and benefits occur at the end of each year in which they occur. This approach exaggerates costs while treating benefits as being deferred; the net effect will generate a more conservative return.

Using this approach, the benefits and cost lines would be treated as follows:

	Year 1	Year 2	Year 3	Year 4	Year 5	Total
Net improvement	0	2.0	3.4	3.9	4.1	13.4
Applied Year	1	2	3	4	5	
Discount factor present worth	.87	.76	.66	.57	.50	
Present worth	0	1.5	2.2	2.2	2.1	8.0

	Year 1	Year 2	Year 3	Year 4	Year 5	Total
Net costs	(1.5)	(.7)	(.8)	(.9)	(1.0)	(4.9)
Applied year	0	1	2	3	4	
Discount factor	1.0	.87	.76	.66	.57	
Present worth	(1.5)	(.6)	(.6)	(.6)	(.6)	(3.9)

Net present worth at 15 percent hurdle rate = 8.0 – 3.9 = $ 4.1 million

The rate of return for this project can be derived by a trial and error approach by substituting larger discount rates until the net present worth value equals zero. This calculation can also be setup in a spreadsheet format and solved for directly.

Sensitivity Analysis

Having completed the above calculations, the result forms the base version of the analysis. Financial people often desire to test the sensitivity of the model to different assumptions. Sensitivity improves the understanding of project vulnerability to optimistic assumptions. For example, sensitivity analysis might include the following modifications to the base model:

■ Increase investment by 10 to 20 percent.
■ Defer benefits by one year

■ Dilute benefits by 10 to 20 percent

Each of these calculations can be referred to as a scenario. Typically, if the model can be driven below the hurdle rate by a change in assumptions then further analysis is required.

After Tax Calculations

Most corporate project analysis is done on an after-tax basis. The difference in the calculation involves three additional considerations:
■ The net contribution is reduced by the value of depreciation
■ The applicable tax rate is used to derive the after-tax contribution.
■ The positive effect on cash flow of depreciation is added to the net present worth calculation.

Obviously, these differences complicate the analysis and are subject to corporate guidelines and applicable tax rates. For these reasons it is difficult to generalize, and financial personnel familiar with the correct assumptions should do these calculations.

Revenue Growth Assumptions

In the example provided in this chapter, the comparison of automation versus no-automation was done on the basis of an assumed revenue growth rate. Therefore, productivity improvement was reflected in cost avoidance. There are situations where revenue growth should be allowed to differ. For example, if there is a significant learning cure for reps to get up to speed or if the organization for some reason does not want to increase headcount. Choice of the approach should be a function of the assumptions built into the long-term plan.

17

Proving The Case

Many companies find themselves in the position of "proving the case" after the system has been installed. This scenario often arises when budgets are being approved to support the system after it is installed. Even when a system is initially approved on the basis of ROI, senior management will often demand verification that the results are tangible. Attempting to prove the case after-the-fact is not an enviable position to be in; because, the benchmarks or tracking required to measure improvement were not setup at the beginning of the project. When this type of verification cannot be provided, the system can fall victim to political pressure that undermines support.

Whether senior management demands a method of verification of benefits up-front or not, it is wise to build in measurement systems that validate results from the very beginning of the project. This chapter will provide guidance regarding methods for proving the case. It will also provide more input and insight regarding basic cause and effect improvement mechanisms.

Surveys

At the beginning of a project, field surveys can be used to document and assess end user computer literacy and benchmark performance related statistics that are not currently captured by formal systems. For example, the amount of sales rep time required to create and assemble a proposal. The field survey is often conducted during the Needs Assessment phase of the project. The survey typically consists of questions that have specific quantifiable responses e.g. yes, no, average calls per day, etc. The survey can be used to gather information regarding end user training requirements and productivity measures. The results of the survey can be used to guide training budget development, assess attitudes about automation, and establish "before automation" productivity statistics.

After implementation, a similar survey can be used to garner information regarding usage of the system, attitudes, sources of improvement, and current productivity statistics. Even when a "before automation" survey was not conducted, it is possible to pose before and after questions to gain this type of insight.

Identifying the Drivers

The results the organization is looking for have been identified earlier; these include revenue growth, increased margins, reduced cost and return on assets. For most situations, it is not possible to directly link sales force automation to these results; therefore, one must use the concept of *drivers* to establish a logical linkage to changes in results. There are many ways to approach the identification of these drivers, but one ideal method is the use of cause-effect diagrams. Using cause-effect diagrams will facilitate getting team input and gain buy-in from the organization. The next section will provide an overview of how the cause-effect diagram concept can be used to establish an understanding of drivers of improvement and associated metrics for measuring improvement.

Cause-Effect Definition of Drivers

As described several times previously, the organizational results that most companies are seeking can be described in terms of revenue growth, increase in margins, cost reduction (or productivity improvement), and improvement in return on assets. Using each of these performance areas as the objective to improve, this section will provide a generic illustration of how to use the technique to identify the relevant cause-effect relationships.

1. Revenue

The major drivers of revenue can be segmented into the following categories:

- Market Coverage: How effectively and efficiently is the sales person managing his/her territory?
- Account Management: Is the sales rep developing accounts to maximize yield?
- Opportunity Management: Is the sales rep following through and effectively prioritizing sales opportunities.
- Field Management: Is field management creating the motivation and coaching to maximize field performance?

Using revenue as the objective to be maximized and the above categories as the focus for cause-effect, the following fishbone diagram could be established:

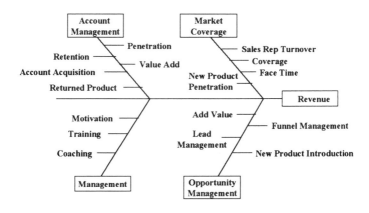

Figure 17.1 Example Fishbone Diagram for revenue growth

Using the cause items within each category, the cause-effect relationship and measurement metric is presented for each item. Note that this methodology provides documentation regarding the assumed impact of each cause and how one could measure this effect as a driver for the improvement of the objective result. For a sales automation initiative, one would also want to document the module or process change that is leveraging this improvement.

Category	Cause	Effect	Metric
Market Coverage	Sales rep turnover	• Erosion of territory	• % sales rep turnover
	New product penetration	• Number of accounts ordering new product	• % accounts ordering new product • % of target accounts ordering new product
	Coverage	• Efficient coverage should increase territory yield • Consistent purchase	• Ratio of actual versus target coverage (%) • % of accounts purchasing
	Face time	• Reduction in non-selling time may result in increased face time	• % face time

Category	Cause	Effect	Metric
Account Management	Penetration	• Share of business	• % share of account's business
	Value	• Customer perceives value received	• Proof of value presentation • Customer satisfaction statistics reflect understanding of value received
	Account retention	• Consistent source of business	• % accounts lost or no purchase • % of accounts gaining or losing volume
	Account acquisition	• New revenue source	• No, of new accounts • % new accounts • % revenue from new accounts

		Effect	Metric
	Returned product	• Selling wrong product or quantity	• No. of returns • % of return orders • % returns to total revenue

Category	Cause	Effect	Metric
Opportunity Management	Add value to buy cycle	• Reduce time to close	• Ave. calls to close • Ave. time to close
	Funnel Management	• Effective qualifying and closing	• Win/loss (%) • Fallout rate per stage
	Lead management	• Timely follow-up on leads	• Lead conversion rate • Cycle time for qualified leads to the field
	New product introduction	• Prioritize activity	• % new product accounts versus target accounts

Category	Cause	Effect	Metric
Management	Motivation	• Incentive to sell	• % sales reps meeting quota • % sales reps meeting quota three consecutive years
	Training	• Skills & knowledge correlated to success	• Ave. training days • % sales reps certified
	Coaching	• Field management development of people	• No. of workwiths • 360° evaluation of manager

2. Margins

The major drivers of margin can be segmented into the following categories:

- Product: Are higher margin products being prioritized and is the best value product sold to the customer?
- Services: Is the sale of services being properly emphasized and is the sales force renewing contracts?
- Value Added: Is delivered value being properly positioned and emphasized by the sales force?
- Account Management: Is the sales force targeting the right accounts for penetration and acquisition?

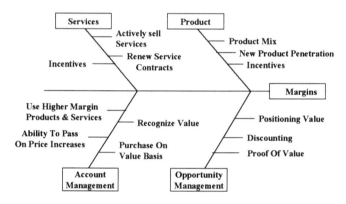

Figure 17.2 Example Fishbone Diagram for margin improvement

Category	Cause	Effect	Metric
Product	Product mix	● Average margin	● Ave. no. of line items sold ● Ave. margin
	New product penetration	● Assumes that new products have a higher margin	● % of revenue that is new product ● % of new product sales versus potential or quota
	Incentives	● Strict revenue focus	● Average margin

Category	Cause	Effect	Metric
Services	Actively sell services	• Assumes that service enhances margin	• Services revenue as a % of total • Share of customer utilizing services
	Renew service contracts	• Leverage revenue and margins on current product sales	• % renewals closed
	Incentives	• Strict revenue & product focus	• Services revenue as % of total

Category	Cause	Effect	Metric
Value Added	Positioning value	• Higher close ratios	• Close ratio • Calls to close • Average margin
	Proof of value (POV)	• Reinforce value argument with the customer	• Number of POV presentations made versus target
	Discounting	• Competing on price	• Average % discount • Line items discounted

Category	Cause	Effect	Metric
Account management	Use of higher margin products & services	• Targeting & penetration of accounts that utilize higher margin products	• Share of customer's usage of higher margin products
	Recognize value	• Is the sales rep emphasizing value concepts?	• Customer satisfaction surveys
	Customer's ability to pass on price increases	• Some industries are very resistant to price increases	• Share of customer business targeted to price

			sensitive industries or markets
	Customer purchases on the basis of value	● Are customers purchasing on a price basis?	● Share of customers purchasing on price

3. Expenses

The major drivers of expense reduction/cost avoidance can be segmented into the following categories:

■

Fulfillment: Many of the tools associated with the sales organization and their support counterparts within the organization can be linked to fulfillment type processes.

■ Training: Training costs for many organizations are significant part of the budget, yet many sales forces remain under-trained. Where is the balance?

■ Administration: This type of activity is non-selling oriented and often requires significant staff to manage.

■ Management: This category relates to the management of sales resources, the deployment of resources, and the effective management of territories by sales reps.

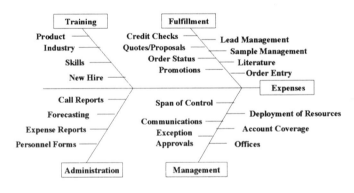

Figure 17.3 Example of Fishbone Diagram for reduction in expenses

Category	Cause	Effect	Metric
Fulfillment	Lead management: responsiveness	• Responsiveness to inquiries typically increases new business and productivity	• Cycle time to send qualified leads to the field
	Lead management: effectiveness of lead sources in terms of generating business	• Improved yield from lead source investment	• $ cost per qualified lead • No. of qualified leads • % of leads that generate new business
	Credit checks	• Sales & support time required to process requests	• Resource time required per credit check • Cost per credit check
	Sample management: Lack of follow-up & accountability wastes resources & impedes improvement in targeting	• Higher sample costs and related administrative & distribution costs	• Sample cost per sales rep • Sample costs as % of revenue • % of samples that result in new business
	Quotes/proposals	• Sales & support time plus production costs	• Cost per quote • Win ratios
	Literature fulfillment: (see comments under sample management). Literature costs also include loss due to damaged copy & obsolete stock.	• Sales & support time plus shipping & inventory related costs.	• Fulfillment cost per inquiry • Sales & support time per request • Costs associated with obsolete stock • Cycle time to deliver literature to the customer
	Order status	• Sales & support time dedicated to the checking of orders	• % time allocation for this purpose

| | Order entry: The implications of order entry go far beyond the cost of entering the order. Often there are checking, editing, & the costs associated with errors reaching manufacturing, distribution, & installation. | • Sales time, support time, manufacturing cost for expediting, change order cost, etc. | • Standard lead-time by product
• Average quoted lead-time by product
• Cost to process an order
• % orders with errors
• % orders with changes |
| | Promotions: These events typically require considerable sales & marketing resources as well as discounted product. The basic question is are they effectively designed, sold, & implemented? | • Promotion development cost, sales effort, and impact on margins | • % targeted accounts participating in the promotion
• % forward buying
• Revenue $ (or %) new sales due to promotion
• ROI or profit contribution by promotion |

Category	Cause	Effect	Metric
Training	Product related	• Cost to create and implement training plus out of the field related costs	• Comprehension scores • Cost of training per rep • Customer satisfaction survey questions • Field management evaluation
	Skills related	• Same as product training	• Same as product training
	Industry or knowledge related	• Same as product training	• Same as product training
	New Hire	• Same as product training	• Same as product training • % turnover due

			• to reps leaving the company • Cycle time required for new hire to be self sufficient

Category	Cause	Effect	Metric
Administration	Call report	• Sales & administrative time	• Cost to process a call report • Field time required to process a call report • Relationship between calls and sales revenue
	Forecasting	• Sales & support time required to process the forecast	• % sales rep time required to support the forecast • % management time required to process the forecast • % support time to process the forecast • Cycle time required to process the forecast
	Expense reports	• Sales & support time required to process the report and enter into the financial system	• % sales rep time required to support the expense report • % management time required to process the expense report • % support time to process the expense report • Cycle time required to process the expense report

	Personnel forms	• Sales & support time required to process the form & enter into an appropriate system	• % sales rep time required to support the process • % management time required to process the process • % support time to process the process • Cycle time required to process the process

Category	Cause	Effect	Metric
Management	Deployment of resources	• The right resource managing the right accounts	• Cost of sales as a % of revenue • Cost per sales contact or call • Customer satisfaction survey • Customer retention
	Span of Control	• Management costs	• Average no. of direct reports
	Account coverage	• Formula for defining the number of reps required	• Hours or calls required by type of account or $ value • Actual coverage as a % of target • Customer satisfaction survey
	Communications	• Telephone, fax, & mail costs	• Cost per rep • Cost as a % of total costs • Cost as a % of revenue $
	Exception approval	• Sales rep & support time	• Cost per approval

			required to process approvals		• % approval rate • \$ impact per approval • % transactions requiring approvals • Ave. cycle time per approval • Customer satisfaction survey
	Offices	•	Rent and other facility related costs	•	Cost as a % of total sales cost • Cost per sales rep supported

4. Return on Assets (ROA)

The major drivers of return on assets improvement can be segmented into the following categories:

■ Forecast: Accurate and timely forecasts typically result in lower inventory across the organization (raw material, work in process, and finished goods).

■ Offices: If the company owns freestanding offices, it may be possible to reduce the number of them.

■ Account management: The ability to target accounts and sell the whole product/service line can impact inventory levels.

■ Revenue: In general, revenue growth should help to increase inventory turns but this is conditional on the predictability of the business.

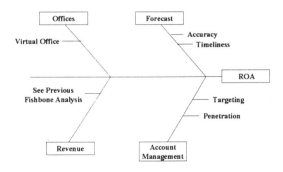

Figure 17.4 Example Fishbone Diagram for the improvement of ROA

Category	Cause	Effect	Metric
Forecast	Accuracy and timing	• Reduced inventory	• % deviation from forecast
			• Cycle time to produce forecast
Offices	Field offices	• Assets associated with the offices	• Span of control
			• Cost as % of sales costs
			• Cost as a % of revenue
			• Value as a % of total assets
Account management	Targeting	• Spot sell product that is in a long inventory position	• Ave. discount level to adjust inventory
	Sell the whole product line	• More predictable sales and discount levels	• % of accounts buying whole line versus target accounts

Customer Retention and Relevant Costs

Customer loyalty and retention are becoming generally accepted and sought after performance metrics. Unfortunately, these concepts can be caught up in hype and over-promise similar to other management concepts such as zero based budgeting and strategic planning.

Although the literature provides convincing proof of the corporate impact of customer retention, senior management will not remain committed to the use of customer retention metrics unless there is proof that retention does leverage superior results **within their** company. Thus, true commitment is gained by linking the concept directly to the company's own performance. On the surface, this linkage may appear to be a straightforward exercise, but it is not. First, one must identify the year when each account was acquired; most companies do not track this type of information. Then, cost factors must be established for servicing the account. Again, this type of information is unlikely to be tracked on an account specific basis. If there are cost mechanisms that track this type of cost, it is most often done on a volume basis (orders, sales dollars, etc.). Thus, the traditional approach to cost accounting does not lend itself to this type of analysis.

These same problems of cost information availability and relevance transcend to sales force automation. Most companies have assumed that support functions can best be managed by simple allocation rules as opposed to understanding the true cause and effect drivers of resource requirements. Fortunately, there is an answer to this management dilemma. In 1984, two respected accounting professors, Dr. Robert Kaplan and Dr. Tom Johnson began to expound the shortcomings of today's cost accounting systems. Concurrently, Dr. Robert Cooper of the Harvard Business School developed a new type of cost system that allocated costs on the basis of activity. The work of these pioneers generated a new method for cost accounting that is called activity-based costing (ABC).

The integration of activity-based costing with a continuous improvement philosophy of management is referred to as activity based management. Activity-based management is a system that links resource consumption to the activities performed by a company and then links those activities to products or customers. It provides executives with an entirely new view of the interrelationship between business processes and customers

If your company has embraced activity based costing, it should be easier to tap into the existing data to define the linkage with recommended process changes. However, if your company is not using these techniques, it may be necessary to set up a parallel set of metrics to monitor or assess the necessary metrics. It is wise in either case, to solicit assistance from your financial department.

18

A Road Map

The focus of this book is on justifying a sales force automation initiative and providing appropriate metrics to support the validity of the projected benefits. Therefore, this section will not be a comprehensive discussion of how to implement a CRM system; rather, the focus will be on the justification facets of the process.

Planning Cycles and Implementation

Gaining an understanding of the organization's planning cycles and their time frames should be the initial task of any initiative because these dates will likely constrain the scheduling of project startup and rollout. It is also prudent to gain sales management input relative to the ideal time to conduct rollout training. This may coincide with annual or regional meetings or it may occur during seasonal periods of lower business volume. Once target dates are identified, one can work backwards to derive the proper milestone dates to make it happen.

Identify Corporate Goals and Strategies

Ultimately, to gain senior management support, the sales force automation initiative must be linked to corporate goals and strategies. Identifying strategies up-front provides a framework for defining assumptions, and critical success factors. Interviews with senior management should occur during this phase to gain their perspective regarding priorities, risk (gap analysis), and establish key metrics.

The Sales Process

Field interviews and discussions with training should reveal whether the organization is utilizing a defined sales process in the conduct of business. If a defined sales process does not exist, then it is questionable whether a rationale sales force automation system can be built. This is a major red flag that must be rectified before proceeding. In addition to defining the process, performance metrics should be identified that tie in with the sales performance and customer expectations regarding quality and value.

Sub-processes

Integrated with the definition of the sales process is the identification of sub-processes that are administrative in nature or directly support sales process tasks. These tasks should be subjected to the analytical techniques outlined in Chapter 10. Study of the sales process and the sub-processes should identify areas of improvement and indicate the order of magnitude estimate of the impact on corporate goals. At this point, interviews or a field survey can be used to provide benchmark data to use in the justification document. Note that by identifying these opportunities as early in the investigation process as possible, provides more lead-time to gather benchmark data to support the claims for the system.

Identify Applications and Costs

Having reviewed the sales process and sub-processes, the project team is now ready to investigate technology. This may include a RFP or it may be at the level of identifying applications and budget level costs. Since the analysis has included the sales process and sub-processes, it is less likely that costs associated with the integration of the system to legacy systems will be overlooked.

Create The Validation Strategy

The challenge for the project team is to be able to show management that the system is indeed driving or contributing to the performance of the organization. In many cases, this relationship may not be directly observable but must be inferred by improvement in metrics that have been shown to be correlated to performance or generally accepted as having this quality. The team must then determine what metrics to use and how the data will be captured.

The Recommendation

Having completed the above steps, the team should be ready to assemble the project proposal for approval. The recommendation should consist of four items:

- **Strategic Overview:** Identifies how the system will support the achievement of corporate objectives and provide a summary of the capabilities of the system. This document may be submitted to senior management prior to the other documents as a litmus test for direction and scope of the initiative.
- **Implementation Plan:** This document outlines the costs and resources necessary to implement the proposed project.
- **Cost Justification:** The cost justification document starts with the linkage with corporate goals established in the strategic overview and develops the rationale for the justification process to a depth acceptable to the financial personnel that manage the capital appropriation process. Obviously, this document includes the ROI analysis.
- **Prototype:** It is advisable to include a prototype of the system. This can be a very crude model. The idea is to take the conceptual nature of the other documents and make it *real* for the organization. The prototype tends to get people excited about the system and helps to establish momentum.

The Pilot

A pilot field evaluation should include the metrics identified earlier in the process. Do the results of the pilot group validate the assumptions built into the system justification? If not, then there must be an investigation of cause and effect to determine the source of the discrepancy.

Post Installation Review

The implementation plan should include funds to conduct a post installation survey to determine end user attitudes and usage of the system. Although some aspects of usage should be available through system statistics, surveys are necessary to gather information regarding use of applications, frustrations, and suggestions. The survey may also capture attitudes or situations that are interfering with the organization deriving full benefit from the system.

The Journey

Sales force automation is a journey not a destination. Systems have a life cycle and therefore must be replaced on a four to five year interval. Management will want to understand the historical benefits received and the nature of the future benefits. Unless each project team follows the disciplines suggested in this chapter, it will be very difficult to satisfy these types of questions. Therefore, each project team must put into place metrics that will assist future teams in their deliberation of the next wave of technology.

Appendix

Assessing Readiness

Is Your Project In Trouble?
The following situations are highly correlated with problems in
successfully implementing sales force automation.

1.   Under Commitment
This can imply a lack of planning, under estimating, or a lack of resolve
on the part of management. In sufficient resources or time frames will
result in short cuts that undermine the implementation or support of the
system inevitably this erodes confidence in the system. A lack of resolve
implies that senior management will back off if there is conflict and will
accept less than 100 percent participation. Since organizations tend to
follow the commitment of its leadership, commitment is key to success.

2.   Selecting Technology Before Defining Needs
Unfortunately, companies still approach sales automation from the
perspective that the technology is going to do the work or make the
competitive difference. The result of this approach is trying to make the
software work after-the-fact. Inevitably, the organization fails to
achieve a satisfactory fit and abandons the project or accepts a less than
acceptable solution.

3.   Vendor Based Needs Assessment
This is really a corollary of Pitfall No. 2. If an organization defers the
definition of needs to a software vendor rather than defining their need
independently, then the solution will reflect the abilities of the vendor.
Thus, the system can be expected to work well but it is unlikely that it
will leverage the true needs of the client organization.

4.   No Defined Sales Process
The sales process is the foundation for any sales automation initiative.
If the organization lacks a defined sales process then the design of the
system will be built on someone's vision or idea regarding the ideal sales

process. When the sales people receive their system, their reaction will be that it does not reflect the way they work. This will increase their discomfort with the new technology and increase the potential for non-use of the system.

5. Minimum Cost Orientation

A cost minimization strategy positions sales automation as something that is necessary to provide the sales force but into something that necessarily adds value. This tends to be a self fulfilling prophesy; very little value will be delivered and use of the system will be limited to the individual motivations of the end users.

6. Sales Automation Run By The IS Organization

There are two basic difficulties with this situation: (a) the end user organization must be committed to success and (b) the end user organization must be responsible for defining their needs. Without this definition and commitment, the IS organization will tend to define the solution based on their perception and convenience. It is doubtful that the resulting solution will be on target or committed to making the system work.

7. No Centralized Sales Leadership

Many organizations are structured as regional P&L's run by a general manager. This type of structure lacks a VP of sales because the GM's fill this role. Although the role is filled, this structure does not provide a centralized definition of sales processes. Each region tends to develop their own procedures that complicate a sales automation solution. To be successful in this situation requires a senior level person to establish a commitment to a common approach to the sales process; otherwise, any solution will represent only a partial fit for any given region.

8. Automation Because Competitors Are (or might) Do It

Projects that are motivated by a desire to keep up with competition tend to assume that the technology will automatically provide benefit to the organization. In situations where no one "owns" the project and where clear expectations are missing, success is unlikely to occur.

9. No Organizational Buy-In

Successful projects require the input, contribution, and commitment of many functions. This support includes IS, training, sales people, customer service, etc. Without the involvement of these functions up-front, it is unlikely that the project will receive the input and support required for success in terms of design and/or on-going operation.

10. Design By Wish List
Often when there is a lack of leadership or commitment, the organization will approach system design on the basis on everyone's wish list. The problem with this approach is that the size of the system becomes unwieldy due to size and lacks an operational discipline or process to integrate the capabilities. Because the size of the system is too large, the scope is reduced and the resultant system lacks congruence and satisfies no one. Users tend to utilize parts of the system at best or ignore it at worst.

11. Inadequate Funding For Support
The primary focus for many project teams is the development and deployment of the system. Often, inadequate planning and budgeting is provided for maintaining the systems and providing help line and hardware replacement services. Lack of support services will undermine confidence in the system and users will cease to use it for key processes. Eventually, the system will be used very selectively and for low leverage purposes.

12. Wrong Vendor
The wrong vendor can imply inadequate technical solution or an inability of the vendor to support the system during its life cycle. Having a well-defined set of specifications, before vendor selection starts, helps to ensure a good fit technically and operationally. The ability to predict the financial stability of a vendor is more difficult. Affiliation with a larger organization is no guarantee; a better indicator is where the company's current is in its life cycle and does the company have the ability to invest in the next generation product when that becomes necessary.

As described in Chapter 3, cost justification must be considered up-front as opposed to an after-thought. This appendix describes other factors that contribute to a successful project. The format for this material is in a self-assessment style. Completion of the assessment should reveal areas of vulnerability either due to organization environmental issues or to unknowns. The intent of this section is meant to stimulate thinking about the status of the initiative rather than providing some type of analytical score.

Linkage to Corporate Goals

Assessment Category	Strongly Agree	Agree	Not Sure	Disagree	Strongly Disagree
• The CRM initiative is referenced in corporate strategic plans.					
• The CRM initiative is linked to achieving specific future corporate goals.					
• The sales function views the sales automation initiative as key to meeting its future goals.					
• The CRM initiative will be justified on a ROI basis.					

Sales automation represents a significant investment. Senior management will often benchmark (figuratively) the investment in sales force automation with tangible investments such as production lines, that have known capabilities. Therefore, they will want to know and be convinced that the system will contribute to strategic goals. Even though a project may be implemented on the basis of strategic need and not be subjected to a rigorous financial review, ultimately senior management will want to know how the system is contributing to organizational performance. Therefore it is desirable to start the project analysis with the intent of providing a strong financial justification.

Sponsorship

Assessment Category	Strongly Agree	Agree	Not Sure	Disagree	Strongly Disagree
• The CEO and/or President or the division is aware of					

Assessment Category	Strongly Agree	Agree	Not Sure	Disagree	Strongly Disagree
and supportive of the CRM initiative.					
• The vice president of sales is the chief sponsor for the initiative.					
• A steering committee of senior level management has agreed to support and guide the project team.					
• Field sales reps and management respect the project champion (tactical leader) for the project.					

Sponsorship is a critical element of any sales force automation project. Bottom-up initiatives are seldom successful due to the level of resources and investment involved. It is questionable whether any project should proceed beyond the investigation stage without the type of support reflected in the assessment statements.

Project Team

Assessment Category	Strongly Agree	Agree	Not Sure	Disagree	Strongly Disagree
• A structure has been established that links the members of the project team to the steering committee.					
• A project manager has been assigned and given authority to manage the project.					
• Members of the project team represent the various stakeholder groups potentially impacted by the project.					
• Project members have the authority to "make things happen" within their functional areas.					

The project team must represent a microcosm of the portion of the organization that will be impacted by the system. The project team must have effective leadership and have the capability to act; otherwise, the team will flounder.

The Sales Process

Assessment Category	Strongly Agree	Agree	Not Sure	Disagree	Strongly Disagree
• The factors that contribute to a successful sale are known and communicated within the organization.					
• A sales process is documented and sales training is based on this model.					
• Management coaching is based on the sales model.					
• There is a common and effective set of terminology that is used within the organization to describe both the type and status of a prospect/customer.					

Implementing a sales force automation initiative without a defined and consistent sales process is like trying to drive a car without a steering wheel. The sales process forms the heart of any system; proceeding without this definition is hazardous.

Organizational Culture

Assessment Category	Strongly Agree	Agree	Not Sure	Disagree	Strongly Disagree
• There is a strong customer focus within the company that permeates every department.					
• Senior management believes it is more important to do the right things than to do things right.					
• Problem solving is conducted on a "find the root cause" type of mentality.					
• Management wishes to retain quality people and provides an environment					

for personal growth.					

These statements regarding culture are consistent with an organization that employs effective problem resolution. Strongly agree checks in this area suggest that the organization will embrace a well-organized and researched initiative. Low scores suggest that cost and speed of implementation may overshadow quality considerations associated with the initiative.

The reader may wish to use these questions with senior management and other members of the project team. Another source of this type of assessment information is the Audit Standards, published by the Sales Automation Association (see bibliography).

Bibliography

Cortada, James W. *TQM for Sales and Marketing Management*, New York: McGraw-Hill, Inc., 1993.

Kaplan, Robert S. and Norton, David P. *The Balanced Score Card*, Boston: Harvard Press, 1996.

Lowenstein, Michael W. *Customer Retention*, Milwaukee: ASQ Quality Press, 1995.

McMahon, Timothy. *Solving the Sales Manager/Sales Automation Equation*, Chicago: The Dartnell Corporation, 1996.

Moriarty, Rowland T. and Swartz, Gordon S. *Automation to Boost Sales and Marketing*, Harvard Business Review, January-February 1989, 100-108.

Petersen, Glen S. *High Impact Sales Force Automation*, Boca Raton: St. Lucie Press, 1997.

Reichheld, Frederick F. *The Loyalty Effect*, Boston: Harvard Free Press, 1996.

Sales Automation Association. *Sales Automation Excellence Program and Audit Standards*, Chicago: Sales Automation Association, 1994.

Selden, Paul H. *"Calculating the Real Return of Sales Automation"*, Sales Process Engineering and Automation, March 1995, 9-16.

Selden, Paul H., *Cost-Benefit Analysis & Sales Automation*, Kalamazoo: The Selden Companies, 1995.

Selden, Paul H., *Guide To Implementing Sales Automation*, Chicago: Sales Automation Association, 1994.

Selden, Paul H., *Sales Process Engineering*, Milwaukee: ASQ Quality Press, 1997.

Smith, George A. Jr. *Sales Productivity Measurement*, Milwaukee: ASQ Quality Press, 1995.

Smith, George A. Jr. *The Sales Quality Audit*, Milwaukee: ASQ Quality Press, 1995.

Stowell, Daniel M. *Sales, Marketing and Continuous Improvement*, San Francisco: Jossey-Bass Publishers, 1997.

Welch, Cas and Geissler, Pete. *Applying Total Quality to Sales*, Milwaukee: ASQ Quality Press, 1995.

Welch, Cas and Geissler, Pete. *Bringing Total Quality to Sales*, Milwaukee: ASQ Quality Press, 1992.

Professional Organizations

American Society for Quality (ASQ)
611 East Wisconsin Ave.
Milwaukee, WI 53201
800-248-1946

Customer Relationship Management Association (CRMA)
Formerly Sales Automation Association (SAA)
204 Andover St.
Andover, MA 01810
978-470-8608

National Account Management Association (NAMA)
150 N. Wacker Drive
Suite 960
Chicago, IL 60606
312-251-3131

National Association of Purchasing Management (NAPM)
PO Box 22160
Tempe, AZ 85285
800-888-6276

Sales & Marketing Executives
5500 Interstate North Parkway
Suite # 545
Atlanta, GA 30328
800-999-1414

Index